The BAPTIST WAY of LIFE

The BAPTIST WAY of LIFE

BROOKS HAYS
JOHN E. STEELY

PRENTICE-HALL, INC.
Englewood Cliffs, New Jersey

The Baptist Way of Life
by Brooks Hays and John E. Steely

© 1963 by PRENTICE-HALL, INC.

LIBRARY OF CONGRESS CATALOG CARD NUMBER: 63-16742

Prentice-Hall International, Inc.
(*London, Tokyo, Sydney, Paris*)
Prentice-Hall of Canada, Ltd.
Prentice-Hall de Mexico, S.A.

Printed in the United States of America

T-05550

First Printing .... September 1963

FOREWORD

I am happy to be associated with Dr. John E. Steely in the preparation of this book. It represents our joint efforts only in a very general sense. His contribution has been so much greater than mine that I take this opportunity to make clear my junior position on the team. I can take credit, however, for inducing him to become a co-author, after the publisher had invited me to participate in this series which sets forth the distinctive ways of American religious denominations. As indicated in the following pages, Baptists are noted for the recognition given laymen. I hope, therefore, that my contribution as a layman is appropriate. I have tried to share certain views and experiences which I regard as somewhat typical. The elements of scholarship are to be credited to Dr. Steely.

I have a deep sentiment for my Baptist ties. I recall hearing Dr. S. L. Stealey (who brought John Steely and me together) say, "If the Baptists and I are ever separated, they will leave me—I will never leave them." I can make the same claim. And yet I openly admit my "ecumenicity," a term not particularly popular with Baptists. That I may do this without jeopardizing my status is one of myriad proofs of our individualism and independence. While Baptists are noted for their strong group loyalty, they are also distinguished by a willingness to be the objects of the other fellow's humor, provided it is held to the limits of reverence. This Baptist sense of humor is related to our frontier heritage and is used in our meetings "to make a point." One illustration is the strategy suggested by one of our own members. "When you deal with Baptists, don't forget we are independent and a mite stubborn. When you're handling a mule, you don't put him in the lot where you want him. You put him in the 'j'ining lot and let him jump over the fence to where you want him."

My boyhood days were spent in Russellville, Arkansas, in what some would call a circumscribed area—a quadrangle bounded by lines moving from the Baptist church to the courthouse, to the public school, and thence to our little home which my father bought in 1903 for $1,000. Our church, like most Baptist churches, had a considerable number of meetings throughout the week. Our family attended most of them. I could sympathize with the New England couple who moved to a southern town and, finding their own church not represented in the community, "shopped around," finally joining another church. Our Baptists were disappointed not to be chosen. When one Baptist lady expressed this feeling, the newcomer said, "Well, my husband and I would have enjoyed being Southern Baptists but we decided we just weren't physically equal to it."

I remember carrying a lantern to Wednesday night prayer meetings in the pre-electric light era. Lighting for evening services in the little church house was always by kerosene lamps. In these pages Dr. Steely and I have tried to preserve the flavor of the frontier which has contributed so much to our Baptist heritage. The life of western Arkansas for the period of my boyhood is reflected, I presume, in both my political philosophy and my religious convictions. There was, indeed, quite a struggle over the direction I would take—would Church or State have my talents? "The Church won that argument," one of the Baptists said, "so Brooks went into politics." I am under a heavy debt for the congregation's instruction and its demonstrations in democratic government. It impressed me with the need for putting moral content into the political programs to which I would later attach myself. The precious values bound up in the life of every individual were first held before me in that congregation.

It was the example of the local church that produced my first interest in the processes of democracy and the principles of equality. The woman who did my mother's washing shared the same pew with us, not by invitation, but by the right and status accorded by the congregation. She could not give as much to the church collections as my father, and she could not preside over the ladies' aid society as did my mother, but in the congregational voting her voice had the same weight as theirs. The blacksmith to whom I took our faithful mare, Dolly, for new shoes was one of my Sunday School teachers. He, too, was unlettered. From him I learned that the past tense of help is *holp*. "The little boy Samuel holp the priest Eli," he told our junior class of boys. He, too, participated in the church in the same spirit of equality with my father. And a coal miner was another Sunday School instructor who influenced me. His scarred hands, burned in a mine fire, remain for me a symbol of our Baptist concern for "the common people"—for "all the people," as we prefer to say.

The opening of Baptist forums to the laity and the tolerating of nonprofessional teaching is an admirable quality in our Baptist life, but it poses problems. Since all ecclesiastical authority vests in the congregation (a concept which I fear we may have overworked), we find it easy sometimes in the denominational counsels to make concessions to mediocrity.

And while our national prosperity enables Baptists to establish and maintain modern facilities which we did not have in "the poor days," many members recognize that the pressures against our exerting a prophetic leadership are often increased with wealth and the conservative viewpoint which it generally encourages. Our famous Dallas preacher, George W. Truett, used to tell about a written request from an anonymous member of his congregation, "Pray for a young man getting rich very fast." There are some of us today who believe that prayers should be offered for a great denomination that is getting rich very fast. But the conscience of Baptists keeps prodding us, and it will not be surprising to see a more positive response to the recurring appeals for an adequate social expression of the gospel in the dynamic twentieth century.

The political ferment of the times understandably makes an impact upon our denominational life. In an earlier period there was sometimes a rather crude exploitation of Baptist loyalties in political affairs. For example, one Southern politician made considerable capital out of what he called his "simple creed." He never tired of saying, "I believe in paying your honest debts, saving your seed potatoes and baptism by total immersion." Baptist bodies have often officially renounced political interests, but at the same time have activated the membership when convinced that "moral issues" were involved. In the complex modern society there are progressive programs sponsored by Baptist convention agencies for gearing our immense resources to present day needs.

On these points we have tried to avoid editorializing, but both Dr. Steely and I are hopeful that our Baptist tradition will prove itself to be socially dynamic and that there will be positive evidence that our witness is a relevant and compelling one. A noticeable trait of Baptists is denominational pride, and among the marks of progress which we like to mention are the scores of fully accredited senior colleges which are helping to provide a maturing intellectual life for our young people in nearly every part of the United States. This source of leadership is a favored object of Baptist philanthropy.

Our story of the Baptists should make it clear that laymen are honored with a voice in Baptist assemblies and an influence in the main decisions not accorded them in many of the other large denominations. This policy sometimes gives rise to controversy. The fear is occasionally entertained that professional judgments are not sufficiently honored. It is undoubtedly true that our church governmental forms and practices make for rather conventional interpretations of the gospel and at times tend to discourage adventurous preaching. Still, Baptists continue to struggle toward a strong moral position on basic issues confronting the whole society of which they are a part. They are hopeful that their Biblical faith, to which all pay homage, will survive any strains of conflicting interpretations. The literalists among us sometimes fear that the independence of which we all boast may lead to an erosion of that faith. But most of us view the tensions that grow out of these conflicts as a part of the price we must pay for our freedom. Some are more grieved than others that fragmentation occasionally results from our inability to harmonize our differences, but there is an amazing resiliency in the present day Baptist organizations. Dr. Steely and I optimistically look forward to improvements in the technique of reconciliation, which is a mission we reverence, and at the same time, to the raising of prophetic voices in a way that is in keeping with our history and tradition.

BROOKS HAYS,
Washington, D. C.

CONTENTS

PREFACE

The most casual student of Baptists and their way of life will be impressed by the great diversity existing within this family called by a common name. This diversity is often a source of bewilderment to those outside the group. Baptists themselves are not always sure of the lines of kinship, the divergent emphases and the organic relationships within the denomination as a whole.

One who shares through personal commitment in this richly varied heritage feels both delight and despair as he reflects upon it and seeks to interpret it to others. The course pursued in this book represents the best efforts of the authors to do justice to the areas of diversity. At the same time, the unities which Baptists enjoy with one another and with all of Christendom are of primary concern.

This book takes its place in a series prepared for the general reader rather than for the specialist in denominational history. It is to be expected, therefore, that the specialist will be aware of many omissions, some of which may appear to him grievous and inexcusable. Those inclined to be impatient with any such deficiencies are asked to consider the broad purpose of the book.

An introduction to a "way of life" calls for some description of the people whose way this is, and some account of the dominant influences in their common life and thought. This is attempted in Part I, in response to the question, "Who are the Baptists?" Such an understanding is best achieved in the context of a historical account, especially an account of beginnings. Hence we begin by telling of the beginnings of Baptists, and follow this with a less detailed narrative of their general developments in more recent times.

The special "way" of a denomination is, in part, their distinctive understanding of the Christian "way." In Part II we have sought to describe this understanding as held by the Baptists. It involves not only the personal Christian experience, but also the experience of worship, the practice of the ordinances and the demands of obedience, integrity and compassion in ethical choices.

Part III is devoted to a description of how Baptists do their work, both within the local congregation and in the larger fellowship of Baptists. Here special attention is given to the agencies of evangelism and education, and of missionary and charitable work through which they have given concrete evidence of their experience.

Finally, in Part IV, Baptist contributions to the Christian world are considered. While these have not been insignificant in other areas, it is in the matter of religious liberty that the witness of Baptists has been most powerful, constant and persuasive. Thus the book concludes with a description of the conviction with which the Baptists of seventeenth century England set out on their pilgrimage.

The story of modern Baptists begins in England. Today Baptists are found in the greatest numbers in the United

States of America, but are also present in New Zealand, Nigeria and Soviet Russia, as well as in other countries. Both of the authors of this work have their roots in the Southern Baptist Convention in America; and since this book is published for American readers, it is fitting that the central consideration be the Baptists in America. That less attention is paid to Baptists in other lands does not suggest a lack of appreciation for their unique contributions to the life of the whole denomination and to all of Christendom.

One of the earliest expressions used to describe the Christian calling was "the Way." There are very good reasons for that description. It points to the manner of life growing out of the religious theory. Some of the most notable distinguishing marks of the earliest followers of Jesus were in the realm of personal morality and in the sharing of life and work. They shared in the apostles' teaching and fellowship, in the breaking of bread and in prayers. The defenders of Christianity against *literary* criticism, official persecution and general antagonism portrayed a wholesome and unblamable way of life as characteristic of their company.

Within the company of Christian believers there are many communities, each partaking of the life of the whole, yet making its own special and unique contribution to that life. Sharing a particular concern or set of concerns, and experiencing the Christian life in distinctive patterns of worship and forms of piety, these have a "way" of their own. The fruits of their labors and the benefits of the peculiar insights may and indeed should be enjoyed by the whole body of Christ, while the members of the communion alone are privy to the ways by which these labors are performed and these insights are gained and treasured.

Baptists belong to that branch of the Christian family commonly known as Protestants. They share with Lutherans, Presbyterians, Anglicans and others many of the gains (and many of the losses) of the sixteenth century Reformation of

the western Church. In that great upheaval the apparent unity
of western Christendom became a clearly divided group of
churches, each seeking to establish itself and to gain agreement with its position. On the one side, those who remained
in communion with Rome achieved, through massive efforts
at reform and recovery, a closer unity than had been known
before, though on a smaller scale. On the other hand, the
various Protestant churches were unable to find the ground
of agreement among themselves on which they could build
together. Yet, although they could not achieve an organic
unity, they shared some key ideas. Some of these, such as the
priesthood of all believers, justification by faith, the authority
of the Scriptures and the rejection of Roman supremacy in
spiritual matters, the Baptists have shared along with other
later Protestants.

Thus Baptists owe a continuing debt to the representatives of the "main stream" of the Reformation, especially to
the reforming labors and the theological affirmations of Luther
and Calvin. Some of the more specific ideas and emphases,
however, we owe to certain ones of the more radical reformers,
representatives of the so-called "left wing" of the Reformation. The precise measure of their influence upon Baptists is
subject to dispute. Most church historians would agree, however, that Baptist origins are to be sought in the part of western Christendom of the sixteenth and seventeenth centuries
which sought to go beyond and to complete the work of the
major reformers.

This part of our Baptist heritage will make relevant a further word about the character of this book. It may be argued
that a work of this kind ought to be written in a serious vein
throughout, and that the light touch is a kind of admission of
frivolity to sacred precincts. But religious experience has two
focal points: the lofty spiritual truths which it knows and proclaims, and the common life of the people which it pervades.
The music of the oratorio is expressive of these exalted truths,

but folk songs may be employed to express the common religious experience of the people. In the same way, while solemn declarations, formal statements of doctrine and sober narrative may help to illumine the spiritual realities, homely stories may rightly be used to depict the common life of the believer and his enjoyment of that word of life which comes to him from God.

PART I

WHO ARE
the BAPTISTS?

INTRODUCTION

No people are really understood until their history is known. It is not within the scope of this book to tell the detailed history of Baptists, but it seems worth our while to sketch the story to show the course of our development. Thus we may show and explain the influences that have been most powerful in shaping the life of the denomination.

In response to our question, "Who are the Baptists?" some observers may say, "Oh, yes, they are the people who practice baptism by immersion." Others will say, "They are the ones who believe in a local independent church government." Still others may call attention to our insistence upon fidelity to the New Testament for faith and practice. But none of these tells the whole story.

Baptists are a free church people. We not only advocate a church free from governmental interference, but insist also that the state must be free from church domination. Our local

1

congregations are free, too, though they have yielded this freedom in varying degrees to the larger fellowship for the sake
of fellowship and effectiveness in witnessing.

We are evangelical Protestants. We stress personal religious experience and individual commitment of self to God
—sometimes, it must be admitted, to the neglect of the
Church and of the corporate experience of the believers.

Baptists are people of the Book. Almost without exception
our statements of practice and confessions of faith stress our
reliance upon the New Testament (not meaning thereby to
abandon the Old Testament) as the "sufficient and authoritative rule for faith and practice." Our understanding of the
Biblical patterns, in fact, is decisive for us in the matters of
church polity, baptism and religious experience, which are
the external marks by which we are chiefly known.

There are three major epochs in Baptist history, in each
of which we have encountered powerful influences that have
helped to shape our course of life. The first of these is that
in which Baptists first appeared. We have already indicated
that our people arose in the setting of early seventeenth century English Puritanism. The thrusts and counter-thrusts of
church and state, king and bishops, reform and restoration,
molded the situation and formed a challenge to which Baptists were a part of the response. In Chapter 1 we shall trace
this story briefly.

The second epoch came when the young fellowship
faced the demands of a frontier situation in the eighteenth
and nineteenth centuries. The main part of this story is set
on the North American continent, but there were similar
challenges on the frontiers of liberty and opportunity in other
lands as well. This is the subject of Chapter 2.

The third epoch is still in progress. It is the story of the
bewildering and fast-moving twentieth century, which poses
staggering questions and great demands for other religious
bodies, too, and indeed for every structure of our society and

every area of thought. Here are the rising young nations; the advances in technology; new techniques in communication; philosophical and political challenges; the struggles between totalitarian and democratic forms of society; the population explosion, and the rising level of education among our people. Chapter 3 tells the story of how Baptists have responded up to now to these complex and thrilling developments and demands and of the inner developments of our fellowship in this present century.

Such a sketch of our history may prepare the reader to grasp the Baptist interpretation of the Christian way and to appreciate our efforts to put this understanding into practice.

BAPTIST BEGINNINGS

There is no absolute virtue in humble origins. Meanness of soul and pettiness of spirit may dwell in huts as well as in mansions. When Baptists speak of their lowly beginnings, they claim no special favor because of these humble circumstances. Nor are they alone in this experience. Other groups have also begun in the midst of difficulties. The early Christian movement made its way against great opposition from several quarters. Methodists, Lutherans, Presbyterians, all began their distinctive life and work under adverse conditions. Indeed, it is quite exceptional for a new religious movement to begin under favorable auspices or with the support of prominent patrons.

Not only are we forbidden to glory in this experience because it is not uniquely ours, but we must confess that we would not have chosen such a beginning, if we had had any choice in the matter. Few would relish the official disfavor, public scorn, legal disabilities and other handicaps belonging to such a lowly beginning as ours. In alluding to these conditions, then, we intend simply to say that Baptists first appeared as a small and unheralded company who had to make their way against unfavorable conditions and general disapproval.

VARIOUS THEORIES

One school of Baptist historians has sought to trace our ancestry back to the continental Anabaptists of the sixteenth century. The steadfastness and heroism of these men and women who saw with burning clarity the issues in the struggle between the great reformers and the Roman church would be a worthy inheritance for any people. They hoped in vain for the reformers to carry through to the logical conclusion their basic principles of justification by faith and the sole authority of the Scriptures. When these hopes failed, some of the Anabaptists turned to more radical expressions of dissent from the established church order.

The brightest hopes for these people appeared first in Switzerland, where Ulrich Zwingli was engaged, in the third decade of the sixteenth century, in bringing Zurich into the Protestant fold. His earlier sermons and declarations appeared to embody the same ideals which these Anabaptists held, and they relied on him to carry through the reform of the Church with vigor. To their dismay, however, he stopped short of the implementation of his principles, and the Anabaptists felt constrained to denounce him and to proceed on their own initiative to the establishment of true reform. This meant, in their view, an actual reformation of the Church to include only regenerate members who had been baptized on the basis of a personal confession of faith. Since the baptism of infants did not fulfill this requirement, they began early in 1525 the practice of believers' baptism (or, as their opponents called it, re-baptism; hence the name *ana*-baptists, re-baptizers). The reaction of the authorities was quick and harsh. The death of such responsible leaders as Balthasar Hubmaier, Conrad Grebel and Felix Manz left the young movement in the hands of more radical reformers, men who were less able and less responsible.

Frustration of Anabaptist hopes in various places led finally to the tragic episode of Muenster in Westphalia, Germany. Here a group of the radicals sought to establish a theocratic kingdom, a new Jerusalem. Almost unbelievable excesses resulted. Finally, in 1535, Catholic and Lutheran forces joined to end the experiment by force of arms.

The Muenster episode was disastrous for the Anabaptist cause before its bloody culmination, for the opponents of the cause were quick to point to the excesses as the inevitable result of Anabaptist principles. The surviving members were scattered, and the name became an epithet more despised than before. When the first English Baptists emerged, critics sought to identify them with the discredited continental Anabaptists. Later, beginning in the middle of the eighteenth century, some Baptist historians claimed a connection with moderate Anabaptists. Yet, the General Baptist Confession of 1611 had named and rejected some views common to Anabaptists, as if to distinguish themselves from the earlier group. Both the General Baptist Confession of 1660 and the Particular Baptist Confession of 1644 specifically rejected the identification of their movement with the Anabaptists.

Other students of Baptist history have tried, with even less justification, to trace the Baptist lineage through various dissenting sects of the Middle Ages and the early Church back to apostolic times. In some of their accounts, Baptists have been virtually identified with Waldensians, Albigensians, Cathars, Paulicians, Bogomils, and Montanists. The fact that for one reason or another these groups dissented from the teaching or practice of the Church of their day seemed reason enough to connect them with modern Baptists. Through a

clearer and fuller understanding of the groups and their doctrines than was possible in earlier times, these attempts today
are largely discredited. It may safely be said that there is no
organic connection between them and modern Baptists, and
that any kinship between the two is limited to an occasional
similarity of emphasis, either positive or negative. These people are not the forebears of the Baptists.

Yet, Baptists, like all free churchmen, are heirs of these
and of all others who kept alive the spirit of dissent and thus
fostered the spirit of freedom. It ought to be said without
condescension that Baptists recognize the merits and profit
from the insights which these people possessed, honor them
for their achievements, and study them with great interest.

THE ENGLISH CHURCH UNDER THE TUDORS

The ordering of the Church's life in England was subject
to royal whims in the days of Henry VIII. In the 1530's the
king was acknowledged to be the "Supreme Head" on earth
of the Church in England and the supreme authority of the
bishop of Rome was rejected. Protestant principles, however,
were not thereby established. By the end of Henry's reign in
1547, no clear Protestant pattern for the Church was evident.
A few steps in the direction of a more definite Protestantism
were taken during the brief reign of young Edward VI. When
his half-sister Mary, daughter of Henry and the Catholic
Catherine of Aragon, succeeded him, Roman supremacy was
re-established.

Five years later Elizabeth I came to the throne and began the long and tedious process of rearranging the Church's
worship and government to express its status, free from Rome,
yet claiming still its full Catholic nature. In the *Thirty-nine
Articles of Religion* and the *Book of Common Prayer* this
"Elizabethan Settlement" was epitomized.

Among the queen's subjects were many who did not endorse the changes. Many were critical because the established

religion retained too many remnants of Roman practice and order. These dissenters held that the reformation was inconsistent and incomplete. They hoped that the church might yet be purified of the remaining signs of a discredited religion. They were not agreed among themselves on how far this purification should go, and some separate designations must be used to distinguish the parties holding differing views. However, the general direction of their efforts earned for them all the name of "Puritans."

Some of these had their inspiration from Geneva, Switzerland, and the work of John Calvin there. These believed that the hope of a purified church lay in a presbyterian form of church government. They did not advocate the disestablishment of the church, but rather held still to the advantages of a church enjoying the special favor of governmental support and protection.

Others were convinced of the rightness of congregational polity in the church. Some of these did not object to the church's ties with the government provided an independent church order could be maintained. Still others, though, saw the continuing episcopal order more firmly fixed in the Church of England than ever before, and these gave up hope of a radical reformation so long as the practice of establishment continued. The true Church could not be co-extensive with the commonwealth but must instead be limited to the company of those who are regenerate. These holding such views began separating themselves from the parish churches and commenced worshipping in small groups, or "conventicles," where only regenerate persons were deemed worthy of membership and where local self-government of the congregation was practical.

The government of Elizabeth I was not hospitable to such ideas. From both secular and ecclesiastical authorities the Puritans suffered continual harassment. Their lot in England was not likely to be bettered. Hope of a better life and greater freedom in the Netherlands led some to emigrate. In the first years of the seventeenth century, at the end of Elizabeth's life, considerable numbers of Puritans had already sought refuge outside the country, or were ready to seek it in case their conditions were not improved by a change in royal authority. Elizabeth died in 1603, and the questions about the lot of Puritans under her successor were not long left unanswered.

BAPTIST CHURCHES' BEGINNINGS IN THE REIGN OF JAMES I

Elizabeth I left no heirs in the Tudor line to take up the rule after her death, so James VI of Scotland, of the Stuart family, was called to the throne of England as James I. The Puritan churchmen approached him hopefully with some of their grievances and aspirations, but the Hampton Court Conference, held a few months after his accession, showed that their hopes were vain. James was thoroughly committed both to an established church and to an episcopal form of church government. He intended England under his rule to provide no room for dissent of any kind.

The migrations to the Netherlands continued and increased. Among the emigrants seeking refuge there were some separatists from Scrooby and Gainsborough in the Midlands. John Smyth and Thomas Helwys were leaders in this company. While in the Netherlands, a part of the congregation under Smyth's leadership came to recognize an inconsistency in their demand for a pure church of regenerate membership while they still endorsed the baptism of infants. They, therefore, settled upon a bold step, perhaps encouraged by the example and teaching of neighboring Anabaptists, and instituted among themselves the practice of believers' baptism.

They did not at this time arrive at the practice of immersion which was later to appear as the regular Baptist form of baptism.

Thus, the first congregation of English Baptists was formed. A few years later, after Smyth had left the group in pursuit of his own spiritual pilgrimage, Helwys led the faithful group still holding to the new-found Baptist views back to England. They settled in London and there established the first Baptist church on English soil in 1612.

While in the Netherlands, these people had encountered the theological developments within the Calvinist ranks in that country. Jacob Arminius and his followers were proposing important modifications of the prevailing doctrinal views. A key issue in such modification was the doctrine of the atonement, which the Arminians interpreted as "general," or efficacious for all mankind, and not merely "particular," or efficacious for the "elect" alone. These earliest English Baptists were won to the Arminian position on this and other closely related doctrinal questions, and thus have come to be known as "General Baptists."

They increased in number and strength quite slowly. In 1640, when the affairs of state in England took a turn that led to the downfall of Charles I, son of James I, and to the establishment of the Commonwealth, there were only five or six General Baptist churches in England. In the twenty years following that date, however, they experienced rapid growth. Before advancing to that part of the story we must return to pick up another strand of the narrative. This is the account of the beginnings of Particular Baptists.

PARTICULAR BAPTIST BEGINNINGS

In 1616 there was founded in London a church on congregational principles that did not include separation from the establishment. It is commonly known as the Jacob-Lathrop-

Jessey church, from the succession of its ministers in this early period. As early as 1633 some of the members of this congregation began actively to question the validity of the baptism which they had received in the Church of England and were re-baptized. It is not clear whether at this time they were concerned with the question of infant baptism, or only with the rightfulness of baptism at the hands of the Church of England, a church which in their view was not properly re-formed. At any rate, in 1638 still another group was dismissed from the Jacob-Lathrop-Jessey church because they had come to the conclusion that baptism was only for professed believers and not for infants incapable of exercising saving faith. The separation was a friendly one, and fellowship was maintained between the two groups.

This group differed from the earlier Baptist church under the leadership of Helwys not only in the matter of Separatism or non-Separatism, but also in theological questions. They held to the stricter Calvinist view of the atonement, believing it to be a "particular" saving work accomplished only for the sake of the elect. Hence they came to be known as "Particular Baptists."

It was this group that first came to the conclusion that proper baptism involved not only a believing subject but also the mode of immersion. In 1641 they re-established this practice. Within a short time this became the regular procedure among General Baptists as well as Particular Baptists.

GROWTH IN THE COMMONWEALTH PERIOD

The period 1640-1660 was a time of upheaval in England. The policies of Charles I in governing without the aid of Parliament ended in his being deposed, imprisoned and finally executed. When Charles was compelled to call Parliament into session in 1640, it soon became evident that a Presbyterian majority prevailed there. The help of all who opposed the king was needed, however, so Congregationalists and Baptists enjoyed a time of freedom. Many of these rose to places of high influence in the army. Oliver Cromwell, leader of the anti-royalist forces, favored an established church. Yet he defended the freedom of all the Protestant groups whom he thought to be politically reliable. Though the Parliament did not approve of this toleration, the personal influence of Cromwell and the power of the army were too great for any effective restrictions to be placed upon the free churches.

The propagation of Baptist ideas was made easier, too, by the mobility of the army. Though it cannot be documented with satisfactory proof, the suggestion has been made that Baptist churches grew up in many communities where the troops and their offices had been quartered and had sown the seed of their beliefs. At any rate, during this 20-year period the number of churches and members owning the Baptist name increased remarkably.

During this same time of the Commonwealth, other significant features of Baptist life also appeared. Members of the churches holding to a similar pattern of belief and practice saw the benefits of fellowship beyond the local congregation, and the first Baptist associations were formed.

A distinct self-consciousness also began to emerge. This was given expression in the public statements of belief and practice known as confessions. Not intended to replace the ancient creeds of the church, these confessions of faith were set forth to present the Baptist case to the world, to disown the name and stigma of the Anabaptists and to affirm the orthodoxy of the signers in the face of mistaken and deliberate misrepresentation of their positions. In employing such statements in their defense, the Baptists were following an example already well-honored among Protestants—witness the Augsburg Confession, the Helvetic Confessions and the Westminster Confession from this same period. In 1644 the representatives of seven Particular Baptist Churches in London expressed their intention thus:

> Surely, if ever people had cause to speake for the vindication of the truth of Christ in their hands, wee have, that being indeed the maine wheele at this time that sets us aworke; for had any thing by men been transacted against our persons onely, wee could quietly have sitten still, and committed our Cause to him who is a righteous Judge, who will in the great day judge the secrets of all mens hearts by Jesus Christ: But being it is not only us, but the truth professed by us, wee cannot, we dare not but speake.[1]

This emerging self-consciousness is evidenced also in the face-to-face debates in which Baptists engaged with their critics, and in the flood of pamphlets which issued from Baptist writers in defense of their Christian orthodoxy, Scriptural correctness and moral uprightness.

RENEWED PERSECUTION, THEN NEW TOLERATION

Upon his death Cromwell was succeeded by his son, Richard, who then retired after a few months. The resulting threat of anarchy brought new dangers to the Baptists, for they had already been charged with anarchistic tendencies under the name of "anabaptist." During the interregnum several fanatic and extremist sects, such as the Diggers, the Levellers and the Fifth Monarchists, had arisen. The renewed danger of being tarred with this brush brought forth new defenses from the Baptists, who were eager to affirm their sobriety and lawfulness. But even this effort did not avail to protect them from the new governmental restraints.

Parliament invited Charles II, son of Charles I, to assume

[1] *Quoted from* W. L. Lumpkin, *Baptist Confessions of Faith* (Philadelphia: The Judson Press, 1959), p. 154.

the throne, and this he did in 1660. There was enough "clear and present danger" to good order in the land to call forth restrictive legislation, and the various acts of the Clarendon Code (1661-1665) provided the legal basis for harsh treatment of all religious dissent.

Charles II was succeeded by his brother, James II, an avowed Roman Catholic. During the first part of his reign the persecution continued, but in 1687 his Declaration of Indulgence ended the active persecution of the dissenters. The next year the "Glorious Revolution" removed James from the throne and installed William and Mary as rulers of England. Their Act of Toleration of 1689 seemed to bring to the Baptists and other dissenters the day of liberty for which they had fought and suffered.

Almost at the same time, however, a period of decline began. The most urgent issues of the day appeared no longer to be religious, but social, industrial and economic. The age of rationalism reached England. The opening years of the eighteenth century were, in fact, years of decline for the Church of England as well as for dissenting congregations. Within a single century, then, Baptists had appeared on the scene, had borne their witness, had grown to considerable prominence, and, it seemed, had burned up the energy which had set them in motion. That this latter judgment was not true is due to a combination of several factors, which will be discussed in the next chapter.

BAPTISTS on the FRONTIER

When a young Baptist pastor left his congregation in a midwestern state to take up new duties in one of the southwestern states, one of his elderly parishioners asked him in all seriousness and genuine concern, "Are you going out there to a place where, if a fellow doesn't like you, he'll shoot you?" This was in 1948. The pastor, it seemed to her, was going all the way out to the ragged edge of civilization and beyond, to the true frontier.

That area is not, and was not in 1948, that kind of frontier country. Yet, it was, and is, another kind; and Baptists have always been a kind of frontier people. Our preachers often moved with the pioneer settlers who opened up the West, and they often lived in biting hardship.

The essence of a pioneering situation, however, is not its hardship. It is rather the unceasing demand for resourcefulness, flexibility and the ability to improvise to meet the new situations. On the frontier, the rigid theorist, who knows only to "go by the book," is lost. The pioneer, where there are no houses, makes a shelter of boughs. When there are no maps, he finds his way by exploration. And even though the terrain is different from that in his former home, he may be guided by the same stars, and may follow the same rules of common sense that have seen him through other strange and untravelled country.

This is a parable of the experience of Baptists. We have always been on the frontier. Yet in a special sense the period of 175 years from 1675 to 1850 forms a special epoch in the life of our people, when we were tested by a series of new situations in which both resourcefulness and stability were demanded.

DEVELOPMENTS IN ENGLAND

The English Baptists of the seventeenth century had hardly had time enough to "find themselves" when they were confronted with a series of critical decisions. Some of these were prompted by external events, and others arose out of changes taking place within the company of Baptists. In all of them, however, there was a danger that the young communion might make a false step and thus betray the principles on which they were founded. There was the equal danger that in trying to carry through to a conclusion these precious principles they might go to indefensible extremes. Both of these perils claimed their victims. It is to the credit of these early Baptists that they managed to remain true to their basic convictions without cutting themselves off from the body of Christendom.

One of the first of these decisions was required when Baptists began to see the necessity for some kind of general organization among the churches. As early as the 1640's the English Baptists began forming associations, and by 1660 these had become permanent fixtures in the Baptist scene. They did not represent a novel idea, since military organization in that period employed the same pattern. Their adaptation of it to religious purposes is expressed in the Second London Confession issued in 1677:

> Article 14. As each Church, and all the Members of it, are bound to pray continually, for the good and prosperity of all the Churches of Christ, in all places; and upon all occasions to further it (every one within the bounds of their places, and callings, in the Exercise of their Gifts and Graces) so the Churches (when planted by the providence of God so as they may injoy opportunity and advantage for it) ought to hold communion amongst themselves for their peace, increase of love, and mutual edification.[1]

Before 1690 both the General Baptists and the Particular Baptists had established general assemblies for a national gathering of those who shared their convictions. The pioneering spirit of those who led in the formation of these bodies may not be evident to us at first.

Still, there were dangers. These people had withdrawn from a church in which external authority over the local congregation was clearly fixed, in the hands of the bishop. It seemed to some that any organization beyond the boundaries of the local congregation must inevitably lead to a renewal of the domination from which they had escaped at great cost. They did not intend to be drawn into an ecclesiastical trap. In order to safeguard this precious liberty, the associations and the general assembly took great precautions and disavowed any intention of ruling the local church.

In the latter half of the seventeenth century Baptists were thrust into another new and difficult situation by the appearance of some differing theological ideas within their own fellowship. Among the General Baptists in particular these prob-

---

[1] *Quoted by* Lumpkin, *op. cit.,* pp. 288 f.

lems were to take their toll in strength and in membership. One of these new teachings was a view of the person of Christ which virtually denied his humanity. Such a view had been taught by one Melchior Hofmann, a Continental Anabaptist, and it was now taken over by Matthew Caffyn, a General Baptist of considerable influence. While the Orthodox Confession of 1678, a General Baptist statement, repudiated the view, this did not end its influence. A little later a different idea, going to the opposite extreme and denying the divinity of Christ, made its appearance among General Baptists. This was a revival of the ancient Arian heresy and of the more recent Socinian doctrine. The General Baptists were less than decisive in dealing with this problem, and many of the churches moved gradually into a kind of Unitarianism until their Baptist identity was lost.

Another theological challenge of a more wholesome sort appeared in the eighteenth century when the Wesleyan revival swept England. There is no doubt that Baptists were greatly affected by this resurgence of spiritual religion. The Arminian theology of Wesley made room for personal decision much more easily than did hyper-Calvinism. At this time the Particular Baptists were in danger of yielding altogether to a rigid predestinarian theology that negated any reason for preaching the invitation of the gospel.

It was not through the Particulars but through a new group of General Baptists that the great revival first made a distinct impact upon Baptist life and thought. Dan Taylor, a rough-and-ready Yorkshireman, had joined the Methodists, but through study came to adopt Baptist views of baptism. He united with a General Baptist church, became a pastor, and shared in the work of the General Assembly. After some years of growing dissatisfaction with the prevailing theological views among General Baptists, he led in the formation of a New Connexion of General Baptists. This group did not have the strong Separatist antecedents of the earlier group, and a more irenic spirit made it possible for them to participate in the revival with other Christians. This spirit was to leave the way open for their final union with the Particular Baptists in 1891.

The Particulars were in conflict with the Wesleys, chiefly over the basic theological outlook, from the first. Yet, before the end of the century the hyper-Calvinism among these Baptists had been modified through the work of such men as Robert Hall, senior, and Andrew Fuller. They were now ready to take up the task of Christian missions to other lands, which was begun with the formation of the Particular Baptist Missionary Society for Propagating the Gospel Among the Heathen. The precise measure of our Baptist debt to the Methodist revival cannot now be ascertained, but it surely was one of the factors in the development of a missionary spirit among our people. It is another witness to the fact that we are not alone in the Christian enterprise, and that we are debtors to our brethren in Christ who bear another name.

BAPTISTS IN THE NEW WORLD

Baptists in America, like those in other places, have been negligent about preserving the kind of records which later generations would like to have. Perhaps the pioneers were so busy making history that they had little time for writing it. It appears, though, that in most cases they gave little thought to either process.

The story of American Baptists usually begins with Roger Williams. This passionate apostle of religious liberty, founder of the settlement in Rhode Island, shared in the formation of the first Baptist church in this country, constituted in Providence about 1638. Williams himself did not long remain in his company. Convinced that his baptism was not valid, because it was not in the apostolic succession, he left the Baptists and became a "Seeker." Yet the seed of Baptist church life was planted, and Rhode Island became a center for other churches. Within a few years another church was formed at Newport under the leadership of John Clarke. The work of Williams in providing a place where religious liberty was guaranteed cannot be forgotten. Baptists should rejoice in having been able to claim his allegiance, if only for a little while.

Not many of our number settled in other parts of New England until late in the seventeenth century. The other colonies did not welcome them. The New England colonists generally had not come to the new world in order to establish religious liberty. Insofar as religious motives impelled them, they were seeking a place where they could establish the church according to the pattern which they deemed correct. They had no more room for those who dissented from it than had the church from which they fled.

Nevertheless, against such resistance Baptists slowly made their way. In Massachusetts they suffered actual persecution and for a long time a measure of legal disability, yet they gradually gained a place there. Henry Dunster, president of Harvard, lost his job and his home when he adopted and persisted in Baptist views. He found refuge in the Plymouth Colony which was not so hostile to these views as was the Massachusetts Bay Colony. In 1665 the First Baptist Church in Boston was organized, and by the end of the century there were several other churches in existence.

A church in Kittery, Maine, was formed with the help of the Boston church in 1682. From here William Screven, one of the leaders, went to South Carolina where a church was established in the vicinity of Charleston. Other accessions to the company made Charleston the first major center of Baptist work in the South.

In the middle colonies, especially in Pennsylvania and New Jersey, the Baptists found even greater opportunity. An atmosphere of toleration gave them a chance to thrive. Ap pearing first in the 1680's, by 1700 they had founded several churches and had begun to form the Philadelphia Association, which was to become the "mother association" for several others.

One of the most decisive epochs in American religious history, not for Baptists alone, was the series of revivals beginning in 1726 and continuing to the middle of the century, known as the Great Awakening. The preaching of Jonathan Edwards, the Tennents and George Whitefield shaped this movement. Though Baptists were not among the most noted leaders, they shared in the effects. Some of the churches were divided over the propriety of supporting the revival, as were churches of other denominations as well. Among the Congregationalists who supported the new movement, the so-called "Separates," many became Baptists, and some of these were leaders in a new center of activity in the Carolinas and Virginia.

Frontier conditions offered special opportunities to a church with a minimum of prescribed ritual. Adaptability to new conditions often spelled the differences between survival and dissolution. No doubt the democratic polity of the Baptist churches made its appeal to the pioneers, who were not likely to accept the rule of a bishop back in one of the civilized cities on the eastern seaboard. The ministers for the Baptist churches were drawn from among the people; they were not a race apart from their congregations. Never present in sufficient numbers, and generally lacking in education, they did not supply what we today would deem an adequate ministry to these people. The handicap of illiteracy in a minister is not overcome by spiritual gifts, but it may be (and among these frontier preachers it was) overlooked by those whose own educational status is no higher. Personal qualities of deep piety, zeal, unselfishness and moral integrity often carried the message of these men more surely and truly than did their language.

The Baptist message of religious liberty seemed consonant with the new surge for political liberty expressed in the American Revolution. Democratic ideals were far from the minds of many of the revolutionary leaders, but they were bound to follow in the train of events. Among the churches, none was better prepared to move in step with this development in political theory than the Baptist communion.

About the turn of the century, after great numbers had migrated to the new lands beyond the mountains, a new revival movement swept the frontier. This Second Great Awakening had its initial stages in the East, but in the pioneer country it reached its peak of intensity and greatest breadth of influence. There it was largely a Methodist-Baptist-Presbyterian phenomenon. It often found expression in excessive emotionalism, and sometimes the participants in camp meeting services were seized by a sense of guilt, or fear or ecstasy, resulting in shouting, dancing or falling in convulsions. In spite of all these excesses, however, the Frontier Revival made substantial contributions to all the churches which would allow its influence in their midst. The real test posed to the churches by the movement was a double one: would a given church be able to utilize the new religious fervor which was created, and would it be able to control that fervor within the bounds of decency and order? Though often failing in the latter part of the test, Baptists showed themselves able to respond to the challenge of religious interest, and thus were aided in their westward march.

At the beginning of the nineteenth century the churches in America shared in the newly awakened interest in Christian missions that was stirring the English churches. Early in the century various Baptist groups formed home mission societies for the support of workers in the pioneer areas and among the Indians. It remained, however, for a chain of unusual circumstances to prompt the Baptists here to enter the foreign mission enterprise. In 1812 Luther Rice and Adoniram Judson were sent out by the American Board of Commissioners for Foreign Missions to India. Both were Congregationalists. On the voyage both came to adopt Baptist views, and upon their arrival in Calcutta they were baptized into a Baptist church there. Judson remained, while Rice returned to the United States to urge the American Baptists to take up their share of the world missionary task. In 1814, largely through his efforts, they formed the General Missionary Convention of the Baptist Denomination in the United States. There was stout resistance to the project. Some objected on theological grounds, the old hyper-Calvinism maintaining that such efforts were blasphemous, since God would save those whom he chose, and the others could not be saved in any event. Others were fearful of the ecclesiastical machinery which such an enterprise seemed to demand. On the frontier there was resentment of regularly paid missionaries and leaders of the mission agency who, it was feared, might "lord it over" the churches. Some were willing for missionaries to be sent if they were ready to go "on faith," without any assurance of financial support.

In spite of the opposition, the Convention grew and succeeded in its basic purpose. At the same time, it not only elicited and combined support for missionary work but also began to develop a denominational consciousness among the Baptists of the entire country.

This fear of an ecclesiastical structure was partially responsible for the loss of some members, and even of entire congregations, from the Baptist ranks in the reform movement of the 1820's and 1830's. This movement, with two converging streams led by Alexander Campbell and Barton W. Stone, drew strength from other denominations, but its greatest number of early accessions came from the Baptists, particularly in Kentucky and Tennessee. Its emphasis upon the primitive pattern of church order and its rejection of non-scriptural organizations seemed to fit well with Baptist concerns. The growing insistence upon baptismal regeneration, however, did not agree with the Baptist understanding of salvation by grace through faith, and a separation was inevitable.

Rising tensions over slavery and related issues divided Baptists of North and South. In 1845 representatives of churches in several southern states met in Augusta, Georgia, to form the Southern Baptist Convention. The old General Convention (often called the Triennial Convention, since its meetings were held every three years) continued to serve as the general agency of Baptists in the North and West. In 1907 this gave way to the Northern Baptist Convention, now called the American Baptist Convention. This group and the Southern Baptist Convention have gone their separate ways, though there are areas of cooperation, and occasional attempts at reunion of the two still appear. In a later chapter attention will be given to the organization of these larger companies, when we consider how Baptists do their work in the larger fellowship.

It must be conceded that our people have failed to respond adequately to some of these challenges. Frontiers of new experience, new social environments, and new religious interest have, nevertheless, provided powerful stimuli for our developing self-consciousness, and the results cannot all be counted as losses. Our geographical frontier in America has been pushed to the West Coast. In the march across this continent our Baptist people have participated, sharing in dangers, experiencing the break-up of old forms and the trial-and-error tests of new ones. Our concluding this chapter on "Baptists on the Frontier" at the middle of the nineteenth century does not imply that there are no more frontiers. The most demanding tasks before our people today are met on another kind of frontier. To these we will address ourselves when we seek to interpret the Baptist understanding of the Christian way, our ways of working together, and the contributions which we have made and should make to the whole of the Christian community throughout the world.

3

BAPTISTS in the PAST
ONE HUNDRED YEARS

Alexander the Great is supposed to have sat down and wept because there were no more worlds to conquer. The Christian church, proclaiming her message in an alien and often hostile world, is bewildered, exhilarated, challenged and depressed in turn by the work that yet remains to be done. Perhaps the word *conquer* evokes the wrong images, but if it is understood as a borrowed word, we may employ it to say that the church has more worlds to conquer than she has already conquered, and she has not the time to share Alexander's alleged grief.

Frontiers seem almost to have been made for Baptists (or, perhaps, it is better to say that Baptists are made for the frontiers). Our work in extending the limits of the Christian community appears to have been especially effective in pioneering regions. It may be that there is a frame of mind among Baptists which is peculiarly congenial to the less formally structured society and the less sophisticated culture of the frontier. It is certain that the Baptists' ways of work and worship are not as greatly hampered by crude conditions and unorganized society as are those of some other denominations. The individualism (often excessive, let it be confessed), the free forms of worship, the non-hierarchical church government and the principle of lay leadership all have served to make the Baptist churches quite at home in the primitive conditions which prevail in new territories.

Yet, within the past one hundred years, frontiers have changed. It is the very nature of frontiers to change by advancing, of course. Other changes have taken place, however, which set the boundaries of adventure not merely beyond the old ones, but in altogether different areas of the world. Still another change has come about. The most challenging tasks confronting any company of Christians today may be in the realm of social and political responsibility within the territories already nominally Christian. For American Christianity, there are vexing questions about the place of the church in the changing city and in suburbia. Serious and not-unfriendly critics are asking whether the day of organized religion is past. Is the Church too much the creation of another age, too closely identified with the evils of conquest and colonialism to be relevant in the newly developing nations of the earth? Is it too much bound up with a privileged class and an old order to have a message for the aspiring and advancing peoples of the late twentieth century? Is it able to adapt to the needs and demands of our contemporary American society while still remaining faithful to its mission?

THE CHALLENGE OF NEW TERRITORIES

In the past century, Baptists have appeared in a score of countries where their name had hardly been known before. Even though we are still more numerous in the English-speaking world, and especially in the United States of America, than elsewhere, the world-wide character of our fellowship is becoming increasingly evident. Nowhere is this more vividly demonstrated than in the stirring ceremonies at the opening of the meetings of the Baptist World Alliance. Here the roll of the nations is called, and those present are reminded of how diverse and extensive this fellowship is.

An eyewitness tells of this event during the 1960 meeting in Rio de Janeiro, where 25,000 people were gathered in the Ginasio Gilberto Cardoso for the opening session:

> As the organ started playing, the procession of flags entered the auditorium at the right side of the large rostrum and circled the entire central ring of the arena, finally entering the platform by a stairway on the opposite side. The flag bearers were seventy white-clad girls from the missionary training school in Rio, each one followed by a delegate from the country whose flag she carried. Many of these representatives wore their national dress, from Burma, India, and Japan, from Norway, Nigeria, and Rhodesia, from Jordan, Bolivia, Colombia, and other lands. As the General Secretary called the name of each country, the flag bearer and the messenger stepped to the center of the platform. The delegate was greeted by the president and then turned to the audience and quoted in his or her own language the words from Philippians 2:11, "Every tongue should confess that Jesus Christ is Lord, to the glory of God the Father," while the flag was dipped in homage to the name above every name.[1]

It was announced in the 1960 meeting that during the five years since the last meeting of the Alliance eight new conventions or unions, representing Baptists in five different countries, had been granted membership. This kind of report indicates the steady extension of an enlarging and maturing Baptist fellowship in every part of the world.

[1] Arnold T. Ohrn, in *Baptist World Alliance: Tenth Baptist World Congress: Official Report*, edited by Arnold T. Ohrn (Nashville, Tennessee: published for the Baptist World Alliance by Broadman Press, 1961), p. 305.

The extent of this fellowship is further exemplified in the leadership of the Baptist World Alliance. The president is the Reverend Joao Soren of Brazil; the vice presidents are from the United States, Hong Kong, France, Liberia, Australia, the Soviet Union, Burma and Argentina. The general secretary is Dr. Josef Nordenhaug, a native of Norway.

The Christian message as understood by our people has taken root in the lives of people in every continent. It is not a provincial message, nor is it the private possession of the English-speaking world or of western culture and society. The establishment of Baptist churches in Nigeria in 1850, New Zealand in 1854, Japan in 1860, Spain in 1870, Korea in 1880 and the Philippines in 1900 marked off further stages of the pioneering Baptist witness which has characterized the past century of our history.

Inevitably the acceptance of the Christian faith through the ministry of a missionary involves some assimilation of the missionary's own cultural and personal heritage. Yet, the very freedom of the Baptist community allows room for the young churches in new lands to adapt what they have received from the older churches without losing the essence of the message that was proclaimed to them. The challenge of new lands for Baptists is not unlike that of the unscaled peak for the mountain climber, but it is more than this. It is the challenge of a commission that sends the followers of Jesus Christ to the uttermost frontier with the good news of eternal life.

CHALLENGE OF CONTINUING TASKS AT HOME

When our fathers met in Philadelphia in 1814 to organize the old Triennial Convention they wisely looked beyond the tasks immediately in view. The chief impetus for the formation of this body was, of course, the foreign missionary enterprise. Yet, in the preamble to the constitution, they stated their purpose thus: "for the purpose of carrying into effect the benevolent intentions of our constituents, by organizing a plan for eliciting, combining and directing the energies of the whole denomination in one sacred effort, for the propagation of the Gospel." The Southern Baptist Convention, when it was formed in 1845, adopted precisely this same statement, but went on to make more explicit the intention to work in other fields as well as in foreign missions: "to promote Foreign and Domestic Missions, and other important objects connected with the Redeemer's kingdom. . . ."

Even so, the wise men who framed these words may not have foreseen the complex organizations which would develop from their modest beginnings. Both the American Baptist Convention, direct descendant of the Triennial Convention, and the Southern Baptist Convention of today have turned their efforts toward an increasing number of new responsibilities since those beginning dates.

The traditional terms of reference for the labors of the churches have taken on a new dimension, one after another. For example, the task of home missions was formerly seen as evangelizing the Indians or ministering to the new communities on the edge of civilization; now we recognize that the missionary task in the homeland may be in the heart of the cities. Both the American Baptist Convention and the Southern Baptist Convention through their home mission agencies are seeking to minister to the spiritual desolation so often found in the city. Among the more than 2,200 churches of the American Baptist Convention classified as urban, one-sixth are in downtown areas where problems of housing, recreation and economic adjustment are particularly intense. It is encouraging to see increasing numbers of such

churches that are willing to face up to the tasks and opportunities of the downtown community instead of seeking an
easier way out. At the same time, of course, there are people
in need of the churches' ministries out in new suburban areas
where most of the new churches are being established.

Similarly, the influx of people from other countries into
the United States has offered our churches new opportunities.
Some of these retain linguistic and cultural ties with their
homelands, and these ties are often expressed in church affiliation. There are conventions or unions in America of Swedish,
German, Rumanian and Italian Baptists. In addition to these,
many churches offer a bilingual ministry for these new Ameri-
cans and for visitors.[2]

Indicative of our steadily increasing consciousness of our
tasks here at home is the list of issues considered for action by
a convention. Even though the resolutions passed by a convention are not binding upon a local congregation, the fact
that they are presented, considered and adopted demonstrates
the interest of a considerable number of people. In recent
meetings of conventions here in America, our Baptist brethren
have taken affirmative action on questions relating to family
life, racial segregation and other discrimination, labor-management problems, ministries to the handicapped, church-
state relations and needs of the aging and senior citizens.

The developments here described are not intended to tell
the whole story of Baptists in the past century. They do, however, illustrate some of our response to the complexity of
modern society and its demands. Still other demands have
been placed upon us by the rapid growth of the Baptist community itself in the past century.

[2] For the information on the American Baptist Convention
in this section we are indebted to *The 1960 American Baptist
Census,* prepared by James A. Scott (New York: American Baptist
Home Mission Societies, 1960).

THE CHALLENGE OF RAPID GROWTH

It is difficult to speak of the growth in Baptist numbers without falling victim to dullness, superficiality and pride. Statistical reports are famous for inaccuracy, particularly if they are taken without interpretation. Therefore, we speak in this section of the number of Baptists only in the broadest terms, and then not to boast, but only to say that this remarkable growth represents still another challenge. It poses the question whether we shall be able to maintain the same values and to preserve the same principles which inspired our fathers when Baptists were a small and quite homogeneous group.

Today the American Baptist Convention numbers more than 1,600,000 members. The Southern Baptist Convention has more than 9,000,000. Other Baptist groups in North America bring the total in this continent to near 15,000,000. Though our compatriots in other countries are far fewer, the diversity of viewpoints and backgrounds which they bring to our common task intensifies the challenge.

While it was not intended simply to deal with this problem, the formation of the Baptist World Alliance in 1905 has helped immeasurably to strengthen the bonds among Baptists of different lands and to allay suspicions. This occasion indeed marked the beginning of a new stage of Baptist history. In the words of J. H. Shakespeare, secretary of that first congress:

> We have travelled far when it has become possible to federate the great Baptist community for common purposes, and as a demonstration of the fact that there is now in existence, and to be reckoned with, a Baptist world consciousness.

Not all of the forces acting upon our company during the past century, of course, have been unifying. There have been disagreements as to missionary methods and policies, doctrinal positions and personal matters which have divided, or threatened to divide, associations and conventions. Local churches have sometimes divided along the lines drawn by these disagreements. About 1900 a number of churches in the Southwest withdrew from the work of the conventions in various states to form the American Baptist Association, insisting upon the "old landmark" position which J. R. Graves had been urging on the Southern Baptist Convention for half a century. In 1947 the Conservative Baptist Association of America was formed, largely of churches formerly affiliated with the Northern (now American) Baptist Convention. Still earlier the General Association of Regular Baptist Churches had formed in the same way, because of differences on doctrinal matters.

The problems of growth have also affected the churches at the local level. The 650,000 members of the Southern Baptist Convention fellowship in 1860 belonged to 8,000 churches; the "average church" (the term itself is not a wholly acceptable one) then had 81 members. In 1960 this same convention counted over 9,000,000 members in about 30,000 churches. This time the average church had a roll of 300 members. Can churches of this size maintain the sense of community which is possible in a smaller congregation? What about the ones that count three, four or even five thousand members? If the sense of belonging to a family, a true community, is important in the church, does not our external success threaten the very nature of the church which we seek to establish?

The problems are not going unnoticed. New interest in the study of the church is being manifested among Baptists as well as in other parts of the Christian world. Stimulating discussions on the nature of the church have occurred in retreats and theological conferences planned by the American Baptist Convention and held at Green Lake, Wisconsin. The curriculum materials published by this convention demonstrate more of the same keen interest. One hears the topic being discussed with fervor in ministers' Monday morning conferences, in corridors outside the convention halls, in laymen's study groups and at coffee sessions. It remains to be seen whether we will successfully meet this kind of challenge. Some have advocated more closely-knit organization as the way to hold our Baptist family together and at the same time to meet the many new demands of this century. Still others believe that our only way to overcome the difficulties brought on by size and new tasks is to establish precise doctrinal uniformity. It is not likely that Baptists in general will accept this kind of solution.

Yet, there is another bond that holds Baptists together. It is their common work. When the Southern Baptist Convention was formed in 1845, the people who joined the new company were united in a missionary concern. Their theological agreement was implied rather than explicit, and they issued no theological statement to identify themselves with a particular viewpoint. After more than a century, and after growth to 25 times the original membership, the common task of bringing all the world into obedient and trusting relationship to God through Jesus Christ is enough to bind us together. This surely is truer to the Baptist traditions than is the uniformity shown in subscription to a formal creed or that enforced upon believers and churches by an external authority.

It seems to the authors that we Baptists in America and elsewhere are still a pioneering people. We find ourselves again and again in situations for which no previously written handbooks or guides will suffice. We live on the advancing edge of the time. Indeed, do not all Christians? Is this not the place to which our Lord has called us? These people called Baptists must be ready to meet these challenges, and any others that may come, with faith in God and with dedication to his purpose for us. If we do this, we shall not betray the honorable heritage that has come to us with our name and our history.

PART II

The BAPTIST UNDERSTANDING of the CHRISTIAN WAY

INTRODUCTION

We must reiterate our statement that the Baptist way of life must be understood as an interpretation of the Christian way. We are first Christians, then Baptists because of a particular and peculiar way of viewing the Christian way in its entirety. Hence, in this part, the authors seek to set forth the Baptist perspective as it concerns some of the most important aspects of the Christian life.

Baptists view Christianity as a way of life, indeed as a life, of worship and obedience in faith and fellowship. Each of the words—worship, obedience, faith, fellowship—has implications that must be drawn out. The primary reference is to God as He is revealed in Jesus Christ. Subordinate to this is the reference to the company of the people of God, by whatever name they may be known, throughout all the earth.

Our central purpose is not to magnify the name or the function of Baptists. On the contrary, we seek rather to bear faithful witness to the gospel; to conserve the essential Christian heritage; to speak the truth in love to the contemporary world, and to re-enact in personal life and in the company of believers the encounter with God in Christ. We believe that we have no grounds for justifying our existence if we do not aim at fulfilling these purposes. We do not deny that other Christian bodies seek the same achievement; yet we are obliged to bear witness to the truth of the gospel as it has laid hold upon us.

The Christian experience must be described in terms of personal faith and fellowship. Baptists have been accused (and the charge is often justified) of stressing personal experience to the exclusion of the idea of fellowship. It is our purpose in Chapter 4 to interpret the experience as Baptists generally see it, and to correct some of the misapprehensions that have arisen in that connection.

Close to the very heart of the Christian experience is worship. It is to be expected in a free church that great diversity should appear in the forms of worship, and nowhere is this more evident than among the Baptists. Yet, taking due note of the diversity, in Chapter 5 we shall try to describe the experience of worship as our people understand it and have practiced it in various settings throughout our history.

Observers have always been able to see some distinctive things about the way Baptists interpret and celebrate the ordinances, or sacraments, of baptism and the Lord's Supper. Chapter 6 is devoted to the subject of the ordinances in Baptist thought and practice.

The last chapter in this part, Chapter 7, takes up the questions of Christian ethics which have been most prominent in Baptist thought on the obligations of Christian discipleship, and offers some explanation of the governing principles by which our ethical teaching has been molded.

The CHRISTIAN EXPERIENCE

Stereotypes are easily formed, and they are only laboriously dissolved. Those that have to do with religion are perhaps most easily developed, since they involve matters that are vitally important to us. Of such matters we all like to speak with finality and definiteness to which stereotype expressions easily lend themselves.

Our own stereotypes about our own traditions and positions are among the hardiest. It would be easy to resort to this method of describing the Baptist way of life and simply to call it "the way of strong and vital personal religious experience."

Like all stereotypes, this one has its beginning in fact, and it possesses enough truth to make it respectable. Rightly understood, the description is valid, and it may be the most apt single portrayal of our Baptist way of apprehending the

Christian vocation. Yet, without some explication, so to epitomize Baptist philosophy may be to falsify with half-truth.

In the realm of Christian experience, as in others already cited, we share with the Christian world at large the language of antiquity. We, too, speak of salvation, justification, sanctification, the new birth, devotion and commitment. We stress repentance and faith. We know the language of prayer. Hymns and gospel songs that reflect the Christian experience tell our story and voice the praise of our lips, though the author may have been Methodist, Anglican or Lutheran. And we confess that all our language is inadequate to describe the encounter with God in Jesus Christ and the new being which we know as a fruit of this encounter.

The early church spoke with a sense of wonder of this transforming experience. Boldly and with imagination her theologians ranged over the whole course of human relationships in search of words and pictures to capture the sense of newness of life and joy which possessed them.

Among the expressions that survived, some became dominant. Systems of theology have been developed, using as a center one of these main themes. For example, the sin-judgment-forgiveness complex of terms has afforded a center for most theological systems. Such a use does not, of course, rule out the auxiliary use of other terms to describe the divine-human encounter, though the others are commonly subordinated or modified so as to fit into the system.

Baptists have not rejected this tradition. Indeed, it remains central with us as with most of western Christendom. Within this context, however, our special emphasis has been that of conversion.

CONVERSION

To speak of conversion as fundamental in the Christian experience is to imply at least three prior considerations. The first of these is that a change in the relationship of the natural man with God is needed. Something is amiss in man which needs restoration. God's intention in creation is being thwarted or hampered. This thing amiss is not merely an occasional slip, or a problem of immaturity. It is rather that the direction of man's life needs to be changed. We rebel against God's rightful lordship over our lives. When we perform noble deeds, even these are stained with pride, selfishness and boastfulness. Something is radically—that is, basically—wrong. And noble deeds are themselves not the prevailing pattern of human action. Inhumanity, hate, violence and deceit are so common as to disturb the brightest optimism.

A second presupposition of the belief in conversion is that this needed change is possible. This conviction is rooted, first of all, in the belief that the world is God's creation and that things are not meant to be as they are. God has a purpose for the world and for men. He has provided a point of contact, or a point of access with respect to this purpose, by creating man in his own image. Addressed to man, as made in the image of God, is the word of redemption in Jesus Christ. This is not a word of judgment alone, but a message that is a warning, promise, demand and gift. Sinful man can be changed.

The third preconviction is that such a change must be vital. It will not suffice simply to have a declaration of new status issued. The spirit of rebellion must give way to one of submission to the will of God. Powerful motives, ambitions and affections rule our lives. These must be changed or submitted to the purpose of the One to whom we rightfully belong. Such a demand is expressed in the words, "Ye must be born again." A new orientation of our whole being is required.

Conversion is often used to designate a single moment in the Christian experience, a crisis time when one makes a decision of commitment that is to have lifelong consequences. Without ruling out the relevance of this usage, we intend here to broaden the meaning of the term. It should evoke the view of a life changed by the free gift of God's grace, to which man responds in faith and obedience.

Since this change is to be a vital one, it then follows that the will of the person concerned must be involved. Conversion by proxy would be an anomaly. The very concept of conversion implies responsible choice, and this in turn means that the person who is converted must have attained maturity enough to allow a basic understanding of obedience and trust. It does not mean, of course, that a person must have indulged in vice so that a proper repugnance for sin in its grossest forms may first be developed. Hence, though Baptists reject the idea of baptism of infants, who have not attained this age of a responsible choice, we have extended the evangelistic invitation to youths who are capable of personal commitment and consecration.

Without doubt this has led to abuses. In some instances children have been coaxed to make a profession of faith which they cannot in any fashion describe or defend. The invitation couched in terms of "Do you love Jesus? Do you want to follow him?" issued to a 6-year-old represents a genuine concern for a child's spiritual welfare; but the response elicited by such an invitation falls short of the promise and challenge of the Christian gospel. Happily, our pastors and teachers are becoming increasingly aware of the dangers of a superficial "conversion," which may actually hinder a responsible choice at a later time. Many Baptists have come to see that, in spite of our protests against infant baptism, we have been guilty of practicing it under the guise of believer's baptism in many instances of children's "conversion."

Is Christian nurture incompatible with the Baptist understanding of the Christian experience? Not at all. The Christian parents may—indeed, must—seek to develop in the child the sense of right and wrong, not in terms of an abstract law of nature but in terms of the intention of God who is like a

Father. The church must contribute its share of guidance as well. This help must be given to the child not only in the form of precept but most of all by example. Home and church must provide an atmosphere that will make possible a personal decision when the age of responsible choice is reached. Genuine Christian nurture leads to a commitment to Christ as the happy culmination of one stage of life and the beginning of a new one. The earlier stage ought to lead toward the latter, not away from it.

Such a view will be criticized by some who abhor emotionalism in religion and who fear that to insist upon personal decision is to create still another stereotype by demanding an emotional upheaval. On the other hand, some may decry this interpretation of conversion as inadequate because it does not make enough of emotion.

We reject the idea implied in such criticisms. Conversion is not to be identified with emotion nor with expression of emotion. There are sorrows that are too deep for tears, and joys which an emotional outburst would only parody. Conversion involves the emotions, to be sure; it involves the whole person. But it is more than emotion, and its validity cannot be tested either by tears of penitence or by shouts of joy.

On the other hand, conversion is marked by the twin attitudes of repentance and faith. These are not to be considered as fleeting events, or spiritual spasms. They are rather to be thought of as abiding characteristics of one whose life is committed to God in Jesus Christ. Such a life will be renewed daily. We do not make the whole distance of the Christian pilgrimage in a single day, nor do we store up provisions for all the journey at the very start. There is a beginning, yes; but one who repents once, thinking to be done with it then, has not really repented at all. Faith that is not renewed in an ever-deepening trust, as God gives us to see his will, is after all only a poor counterfeit of faith.

THE NEW LIFE

Conversion, then, is rightly seen as the beginning of a new life and the continuation of that life as renewed by the grace of God. It will be evident from what we have said that Baptists make much of the personal and individual aspect of the Christian experience. No set of circumstances of environment, no patterns of society however noble, can replace responsible surrender to the will of God.

The continuing Christian life is likewise an experience of personal decision, exercised in the renewed repentance and faith of which we have spoken. We are confronted every day with moral choices. Some of these are momentous questions involving basic issues of honesty and integrity. Still others set before us two conflicting values—true values, both of them—and require us to decide between them. The intensely personal character of the Christian experience is continued in this kind of dilemma. We may seek the advice of friends or family or pastor, but finally we ourselves must choose. The loneliness of great statesmen who must make agonizing decisions that may mean the difference between peace and war may be more newsworthy, but it is no more intense than the loneliness of the young man who must make up his mind about cheating on a college examination.

In stressing individual choice there is the danger that we shall forget that the initial choice was not ours, but God's. Prior to all human choice in the Christian faith is the forgiving and seeking grace of God. He bestows the new life, and it is life in the Church, the Church which is His creation, His gift.

Mistaken or limited apprehension of the nature of the new life has often resulted from a one-sided evangelistic appeal. If an invitation is aimed at appealing to the lowest motives, or to purely selfish ones, there is no room for the Church, and no need for it. "Disaster is coming! Time is running out! Be saved!" may easily be translated into "Every man for himself!" Thus, there is little foundation for a doctrine of the Church, and even less apparent need for the Church. Small wonder that some have expressly denied any place to the Christian community, when the understanding of salvation is so narrow and so self-centered as this.

The life in the Church, to which we are called by God's grace, is a life of fellowship. This, of course, means more than the enjoyment of the company of others who think as we do, or who enjoy the same things as we delight in. When fellowship is limited to such a superficial level as this, it cannot stand the stresses of disagreement or disappointment. The fellowship of the Church which results from, and is a part of, conversion, is first of all a fellowship of shared participation in the call and gift of God's mercy. Resulting from this is another sharing, as Christians recognize their common responsibility not only to each other but also to the rest of the world.

It is also a life of growth. The very use of vital terms to describe the Christian experience implies this, and it is not an accidental use. We Baptists share with the rest of the Christian world the language with which this advance is portrayed.

The most common designation for this aspect of the Christian life among our people is "growth in grace." This properly expresses the fact that the growth itself is still a gift of God, and it identifies the sphere in which we advance. This is not the same as intellectual growth; it may lag behind, or it may even run in advance (but not far in advance) of our intellectual growth.

Baptists in general do not recognize the possibility of sinless perfection in the life of the Christian. We prefer to speak, instead, of the lifelong pilgrimage of the Christian toward that full maturity which is held up before us, and of the corresponding lifelong need for renewed repentance and forgiveness. To be sure, we run the risk of resignation to a level of life below our highest possibilities. Only by taking a radically serious view of sin and grace can we avoid complacency and satisfaction with any stage of growth which we may have attained.

We join in the general Protestant conviction that neither the holiness nor the personal growth of the Christian is directly related to his occupation or to a so-called "religious vocation." We do sometimes carelessly speak of "full-time Christian service," as though this were commitment to a kind of honor-grade Christian life to be distinguished from that of the common folk. But this is wrong; it is a denial of the call and the challenge of the gospel before which we stand equal, no matter what our daily task may be. Every Christian is really intended to be in "full-time Christian service," though one may perform this work as pastor of a church, another as a farmer; this Christian vocation may be exercised as housewife, teacher, mechanic or merchant. There are, of course, some ways of earning a livelihood which are incompatible with a Christian profession, because they are based upon exploitation, greed, inhumanity or disregard for the laws of man and of God. There are still others wherein it may be extremely difficult to maintain a Christian witness. In these may be found some genuine heroes of the faith, whose devotion successfully meets challenges never faced by the ordained ministers of the Church.

This new life is also a life of hope. Since the early days of Christian history men have tried to set forth the purposes of God for all of history and beyond history. Every Christian, indeed, shares the conviction that these purposes of God will ultimately be triumphant. In various attempts to read the mind of God we have often made detailed descriptions of the way things are to go in the future. Most of these descriptions have been based upon an exposition of certain Biblical passages, notably certain discourses of Jesus as reported in the Synoptic Gospels, and the entire book of Revelation.

It is fair to say that Baptists generally have held to a literal interpretation of these concepts and a hope of their literal fulfilment. Baptist groups generally, however, have refrained from adopting any statement that would make the acceptance or rejection of a single view of the matter a test of fellowship.

Our understanding of the Christian hope may be described as an ellipse, one of the focal points being personal and the other general. In the expression of these two chief concerns we employ Biblical language, often diluted, to be sure, with extra-Biblical meaning.

The personal element of our hope is usually couched in terms of personal survival beyond the grave. In recent years theologians have shown us that we have blended the Biblical concept of resurrection with a Greek idea of immortality, and the traditional forms of the Christian hope are being subjected to new scrutiny. Out of this study may come a revived interest in eschatology, which is at once Biblical and relevant for modern man. The other focal point of our hope is based upon the conviction that God's purpose for the whole will finally prevail. For the hope itself is not grounded in confidence in our own abilities to foresee future events but in faith in the sovereign and gracious God whom we love and serve.

The Christian hope is not merely a set of opinions about the future. It is a characteristic of the present life and work of the Christian. Life lived in hope is qualitatively different from one that is "hope-less." This is one of the integral elements in conversion; our lives have been changed by God's grace, so that they are now lives of hope. Our hope in Him is a part of the new life, the eternal life which is already bestowed upon us by His gracious gift in Jesus Christ.

The story is told of an elderly woman who summed up concisely, though ungrammatically, this much of the Christian experience in the following fashion. In a testimony meeting in a rural Baptist church she is reported to have said, "I ain't what I ought to be. I ain't what I'm goin' to be someday. But, Praise the Lord! I ain't what I used to be!"

COMMUNION WITH GOD

The one thing that is essential in this new life of moral decision, growth and hope is that it is an experience initiated by God's gift. Thus, it issues in communion with Him. We cannot be satisfied to describe it in other terms without insisting that they be understood in this frame of reference.

Baptists do not insist upon a single pattern of practicing the presence of God. Indeed, our very basic concept of individual responsibility before God would preclude the use of a fixed pattern to which all Christian experience must be subjected. Thus, even the discussion of conversion and the new life has needed to be in general terms, describing rather than prescribing an experience.

Sometimes the communion with God is experienced in mystical bliss. For some this appears to be the height of all Christian striving, the goal for which the Christian seeks all through his pilgrimage. We do not scorn such experiences, though we insist that they should not run counter to the revelation of God given to us in Jesus Christ, nor contrary to the message of the gospel in the New Testament. We do fear, of course, the dangers of pride which threaten one who believes himself to have private access to the secret counsels of God. This is akin to the danger threatening the church or institution that is deemed to be God's single chosen agency for performing His will on the earth. Baptists have suffered persecution at the hands of such churches which have claimed the exclusive knowledge of God's purposes. We dare not fall victim to the same delusion ourselves.

Yet, according to our understanding of the good news, God has promised to be with His people, to commune with them, and to make known to them His will for their lives. We believe this to be, not a remote and unattainable dream, but an actuality, realized daily in the lives of the people of God. When the single Christian or the company of Christians encounters anew the living God, through whatever medium He may deign to speak to us, then that Christian, or those Christians, must respond in the language of gratitude and praise, obedience and reverence. This is the time of worship.

CHRISTIAN WORSHIP

The ways of worship are as varied as are the religious beliefs of mankind, for they have their origin in belief. Nurtured by awe, the "sense of the numinous," fear, superstition, or hope, the worship experience reflects the idea of God held by the worshipper.

Christian worship is to be distinguished from other forms to be found in other religions. This distinction is more than the mere substitution of the name of God for some other name ascribed to deity by a believer in some other supreme being. It is the recognition of the God and Father of Jesus Christ as alone worthy of our ultimate loyalty and devotion. In Him we confess that we have found truth, life, and meaning. Such a confession as this is uttered in the 100th Psalm, known to millions of Christians in the words of the Doxology: "Praise God from whom all blessings flow!"

And we have come to know Him in Jesus Christ. Our own searching did not reveal Him, nor did we merely invent Him to satisfy our desire to have an object of worship and adoration. Much of our modern preaching of the mission and message of Jesus is surely an expression of what we wish He had done and said, but this much is clear enough: He proclaimed a message of the kingdom whose king is God. Accepting, modifying, and interpreting the Jewish traditions which He inherited, He issued a call to repentance and submission to the heavenly king, His Father. But He did not describe God; He revealed Him. Thus, the Christian world today worships God through Jesus Christ whom, as we believe, God has sent to reveal Himself to us.

This is worship in the Christian church. It becomes an actuality when the people who confess Jesus Christ as Lord come together for the purpose of giving praise to God. Christian worship is not realized in its fullness in solitary meditation or rejoicing, no matter how profound or heartfelt these experiences may be. Its richness is truly known only when believers who share God's gift share also in giving praise to Him. Baptists have been known as stout individualists, but our people have not extended this individualism to the experience of worship. The pathetic and worn-out excuse that "I can worship God just as well on the golf course or in my living room as I can in the church" simply will not do. The speaker shows by such a claim that he does not know anything of the riches of corporate worship. He may be picturing in his own mind, for purposes of confirming his comparison, a church service that is disorganized and even disorderly; and surely it is difficult to worship in such a setting. But the nature of true worship is reflected in the exhortations to praise the Lord, addressed by believer to believer, as well as in the words of prayer which are addressed to God. Jesus taught his disciples to pray after this manner, "*Our* Father who art in heaven . . . give *us* . . . forgive *us* . . . lead *us* . . . deliver *us* . . ."

CHARACTERISTIC BAPTIST WORSHIP SERVICES

It is difficult to describe the typical Baptist service of worship. We do not have a uniform liturgy by which such services are shaped. In almost every Baptist church, however, the service will contain the elements of singing, prayer, reading from the Bible, and preaching. The sermon is usually a major part of the service, as far as the allocation of time is concerned. The Scripture reading, or at least a part of it, is relative to the topic of the sermon. The sermon is almost universally framed as an exposition or application of some portion of the Bible, even when it centers on contemporary events or issues.

The most informal and nonliturgical services among our people usually will begin with the congregation singing hymns and gospel songs. Interspersed among the songs will be one or more extemporary prayers. Then follow the Scripture reading, the sermon, and a closing hymn or song. At this time, an invitation is extended to the hearers to make a public profession of any Christian commitment which they may feel constrained to make under God's guidance.

This kind of service would be typical for many churches, especially small rural churches in America, as a regular procedure on Sunday mornings and again on Sunday evenings. An abbreviated mid-week service on Wednesday evening might follow the same pattern. The same general plan may often be used in a Sunday evening service by churches that expect something more formal and more carefully structured for the regular Sunday morning service.

Now becoming more common, and probably representing the dominant trend among Baptist churches in America, is the Sunday morning service which is more carefully planned in detail. These services do not follow any single standard plan, and each church is free to work out its own order of service. A typical service of this kind might be arranged thus:

Call to Worship (spoken by the minister or sung by the choir)

Invocation

Hymn of Praise

Responsive Reading (the minister and the congregation reading alternate verses, usually of one of the Psalms)

Pastoral Prayer

Hymn of Dedication

Offering of Gifts

The Doxology

Reading of the Scripture (usually a passage upon which the sermon is based)

Special Music by the choir

Sermon

Hymn of Invitation and Decision

Benediction

Some churches go beyond this and seek a close approach to the worship of the liturgical churches. Wherever this is done with insight into the nature of worship and the rationale for the historic liturgies, a combination of the Baptist emphases and the majestic forms of ancient worship may result in a truly worshipful experience for the participants. Where it is done without discrimination, the result may be a more formal service, rather than a more worshipful one.

Members of other churches may be surprised at the omission of some elements which they are accustomed to seeing in worship services. One of these is the communion, or the Lord's Supper. Since Baptists do not follow the practice of weekly communion, we have not included it in the outline of the typical Sunday morning service. In some churches, communion is observed monthly; in others, quarterly. Some Baptists observe the close connection between the Supper and the Jewish Passover in parts of the Christian tradition, and they suggest that the Supper should be observed only once a year. In some few churches there is no regular schedule for the observance, and here it is irregularly and even rarely observed.

The other omission which may be immediately evident is the provision for reciting the Apostles' Creed. Its use is not wholly strange to Baptists, and many would welcome its regular usage. In the first meeting of the Baptist World Alliance in 1905, Alexander Maclaren said in his presidential address:

> I should like that there should be no misunderstanding on the part of the English public, or the American public either —before whom we are taking a prominent position, for a day at any rate—as to where we stand in the continuity of the historic Church. And I should like the first act of this Congress to be the audible and unanimous acknowledgment of our Faith. So I have suggested that, given your consent, it would be an impressive and a right thing, and would clear away a good many misunderstandings and stop the mouth of a good deal of slander—if we here and now, in the face of the world, not as a piece of coercion or discipline, but as a simple acknowledgment of where we stand and what we believe, would rise to our feet and, following the lead of your President, would repeat the Apostles' Creed.

The assembly followed the suggestion and repeated the Creed. It was, as eyewitnesses have testified, an impressive and solemn event. At the same time, it declared that the Baptists gathered there, conscious of the people behind them at home on five continents, were equally conscious of their place within the ancient tradition of the Christian church's worship. Yet, our churches do not commonly use the Apostles' Creed, or any other creed, as a part of the worship experience. It is not that we object to the teachings of the creed as such. Rather, we remember how the creeds have been used as implements of oppression to enforce a uniformity of doctrine. We think of them in this category rather than as parts of the act of worshipping God. We formulate statements of faith on our own part, but recognizing that all theological statements are fallible and imperfect human attempts at framing divine truth, we refuse to canonize ony one of them. Thus, the creed has never become an integral part of the worship service in Baptist churches in general.

LEADING FEATURES OF BAPTIST WORSHIP

The outline of characteristic services of worship in Baptist churches which we have given will not suffice to acquaint the reader who has not worshipped with us with our ways. Yet, one who has visited Methodist, Presbyterian, Congregational, or other evangelical churches will not find the service in Baptist churches altogether new and different. Let us consider some of the features of these services.

1. Baptist church buildings are not distinguished by any special marks of architecture, design, or decoration. If the signs were removed from the church lawns in the imaginary average American community, a visitor would not be able to distinguish the buildings by external features and restore the right sign to the right place. In most instances the Baptist church would share this anonymity. The outward appearance would tell more about the general period in which the building was erected or the general cultural outlook of the area than about specific religious or theological viewpoints. "Sermons in stone" like the Gothic cathedrals are not common in America. Except for some quite old buildings and some daring attempts in modern architecture, few of the evangelical church edifices are expressive of religious experience and insight.

Yet among both Catholic and Protestant congregations new attention is being given to the aesthetic and religious significance of church buildings, and some of the most able architects in America are bringing their gifts and training to the service of the churches. So far as we may generalize on Baptist houses of worship, however, we may say that they are simple in structure, whether small or large. Many of our congregations still worship in small frame buildings, and some of these are one-room structures which are severely plain. In the years immediately following World War II there was a great surge of church-building, and a trend toward Georgian architecture appeared to develop. It is too early to tell whether this will become "Baptist traditional," but there are signs already of a rejection of this trend, particularly in the churches that are being newly established in the suburbs and the younger communities.

In the interior of the buildings, Baptist churches still might not be distinguishable from those of other Protestant congregations. The dominant feature of the actual place of worship is its character as a meeting hall. Baptists generally do not use a cruciform design with nave and transept. Variations from the rectangular shape of the sanctuary have generally been prompted by considerations of economy in making some space do double service for education and worship, and the results have not been inspiring. For the interior arrangement in general, as for the exterior, no basic religious or theological insights have been employed in planning most of our churches, and they are functional rather than ornamental or instructive in design.

The prominent place of preaching in our services is stressed in the arrangement of our sanctuaries. Indeed, we often use the name "auditorium" to designate the sanctuary. It is a place to which people come not only to offer praise to God but to hear his word proclaimed and expounded. When one enters this place of worship he sees rows of pews, commonly arranged in two or three banks, facing the pulpit. In many older churches, some of which are still in existence, it was customary for the men to sit on one side of the room and the women on the other. Often, however, although the elder members of the congregation were separated, the middle bank of pews afforded a meeting place for the young people, and courting couples might sit together in this neutral territory.

At the front of the church, the pulpit is ordinarily centrally located, though a divided chancel appears occasionally, with pulpit on one side and lectern on the other. Behind the pulpit, or occasionally at one side, is the choir, usually arranged so that choir and congregation face each other. Recessed into the wall behind the pulpit, and above the choir, is the baptistry. Often a rural scene is painted on the back wall of the baptistry to lend the appearance of a setting in and around a stream of running water. The communion table, where the elements of communion are placed for the observance of the Lord's Supper, is in front of the pulpit on a level with the pews. This is intended to preserve its character as a table rather than an altar.

The decoration of our churches with art and other symbols of the Christian faith is usually quite simple. The cross may appear at various places in the interior of the building, and often a carved communion table portrays the Last Supper. Most of the symbolic portrayals, however, are in the windows, which may depict scenes from the gospels or the Old Testament, the tablets of the Ten Commandments, an open Bible, a shepherd and his flock, or the cross and crown together. Some of the newer buildings are utilizing the traditional symbols and other forms of art to express our ancient Christian heritage and the characteristic openness of Baptists to new truth and new ways of voicing the truth.

2. The leadership of worship in our churches is also open to variation. The pastor usually conducts the service, though he may be joined in the pulpit by an associate minister or a minister of music. On occasion, the entire service will be led by a layman. During Youth Week, selected young people

are asked to fill various offices in the church, and one of these will lead in worship on Sunday morning.

Because of the centrality of preaching, the sermon topic is usually decisive in the choice of hymns and special music, the Scripture reading, and the general direction of the service. This sermon topic is chosen, of course, in the light of the pastor's understanding of the needs of his congregation and the message which he believes God has laid upon his heart. Special seasons of the year as well as current issues of local, national, or world concern naturally enter into this choice. In some of our churches some attempts are being made to blend our Baptist freedom of worship with a recognition of the historical observance of the Christian year, but no general trend in this direction is discernible at the present time.

3. Worship in our Baptist churches stresses the responsibility and the participation of the whole congregation. The pastor is said to "lead in prayer," and not simply to pray, the implication being that all those present are invited and expected to pray while one seeks to voice the thanksgiving, praise, and petitions of the congregation. Congregational singing, too, is a way of expressing the role of the whole company of believers in the act of worship. We gather in the house of the Lord not as spectators but as participants.

4. The music in our services is intended to evoke a spirit and mood of worship, to offer a means of participation in worship as described above, and to be an expression of Christian praise and aspiration. Most of the songs are sung by the congregation, led by a choir or by a director of music.

The songs we sing are not necessarily Baptist songs. Few songs and hymns, indeed, have been written to express the views that are peculiar to our denomination. Even those which have been written by Baptist authors could as easily be sung by other evangelical Christians. More and more our churches are using anthems, as the appreciation for good music rises Correspondingly, more hymns are also enjoying wider usage

The predominant part of the music used in our Baptist churches is probably still of the gospel song variety. Some of this leaves much to be desired in a musical way, and it sometimes reflects a weak theological view. Yet, even this may be rightly used as a vehicle of praise and exultation. One still hears in Baptist services such old favorites as "Amazing Grace," "On Jordan's Stormy Banks I Stand," "O Happy Day," and "Leaning on the Everlasting Arms," all of which declare the joyous and hopeful aspect of the Christian experience which is central in the Baptist way of life.

It may be revealing to name the actual hymns used in a gathering of Baptists from many lands. At the opening session of the Baptist World Alliance meeting in Rio in 1960, the delegates sang "A Mighty Fortress Is Our God" and "All Hail the Power of Jesus' Name." At other times during the week-long meeting they sang "Blessed Assurance, Jesus is Mine," "Crown Him with Many Crowns," "O Zion, Haste," and "Holy, Holy, Holy." Most of these would be heard in most Baptist churches, at least in the United States, in the course of a year. They symbolize the common bond of Christendom and the bond that unites Baptists around the world.

5. We have already alluded to the prominent place given to preaching in the typical Baptist service. We have good reason for this prominence. Preaching is not an exercise in oratory, not a declaration of a single person's opinions to a gathering of others, nor a priestly act performed by one on behalf of others incapable of the same act. It is rather an act of worship, as believers together think upon God's word and his purposes. It is an act of faith, since the one who speaks is not demonstrating mathematical certainties but is bearing witness to his faith, and the hearers truly hear only if they hear in faith. Preaching is an act of dedication, since the willingness to speak the word and the willingness to hear it imply a willingness to obey the word of God which comes through the spoken word.

Much of the preaching in our Baptist churches is evangelistic. Aimed at the heart of the person who has not made a personal commitment of himself to the Lordship of Christ, such preaching is usually simple, direct, full of Biblical quotations, and specifically designed to evoke decision. It is obvious that this intent does not rule out worship. Indeed, only in a context of worship can evangelism occur. Among the members of the church who profess to be disciples of Christ and who are deeply concerned, therefore, for the life and blessing of others, the claims of God are urged upon those who do not yet acknowledge him as Lord.

Preaching is also instructive, and in our Baptist churches much of this instruction is related to matters of Christian conduct. This, too, can be a part of the experience of worship. In worship one acknowledges that the will of God for his life is good, and he commits himself to find and obey that will. Hortatory preaching, intended to offer direction for Christian decisions, then has its place in worship.

6. What of the place of prayer in worship among Baptists? In a typical Sunday morning service in a Baptist church, prayer would be offered at four different points, each time with a different intention. At or near the very beginning of the service, there is a prayer of invocation. In it the pastor asks the blessing of God to be upon the people as they worship, and to make His presence known among them. Then, a little later in the service, in a longer pastoral prayer, supplication, petition, confession, and thanksgiving are uttered on behalf of the whole congregation by the pastor. When the offering is taken, either before the ushers begin to wait upon the congregation for their gifts or when they bring the offering plates back to the front of the sanctuary at the end of the offertory music, a prayer of dedication of the gifts is offered. Finally, at the end of the service, there is a closing prayer, which may be a simple benediction.

In many churches, members of the congregation are

called on to lead in prayer, particularly in the less formally planned services. There is, of course, no general rule about such a practice, and while it may be quite rare or unknown in some churches, in others it is almost a regular occurrence.

Corresponding to this is the fact that most of the prayers offered in our Baptist churches are not composed beforehand, but are prayed extempore. This may seem strange to the members of the liturgical churches, who are used to prayers written and read for every occasion. It is true that one praying extemporaneously may become so involved in searching for words and in seeking to connect his thoughts that he forgets to pray. It is easy to be so busy thinking about prayer that one hasn't time to pray. It may be admitted, too, that such prayer is less likely to be the shared thanksgiving and supplication of the congregation than is the prayer perpared beforehand, when one has had time to think of the needs and concerns that belong to the whole company. Yet, this extemporaneous prayer may be true worship, for it is likely to represent the outpouring of heartfelt thanks, of deep concern, and of genuine hopes of the individual who prays. And if the congregation is able to join sincerely in these expressions, there is no hindrance to worship in spite of less than perfect language or of unpolished forms of expression.

7. We do, of course, recognize the place of private devotions and family devotions for the Christian. Our earlier insistence that the fullness of worship cannot be known apart from the fellowship of the faithful does not nullify this recognition. One often hears our ministers urge that every home establish a "family altar"—that is, the practice of Bible reading and prayer regularly in the family circle. In the services of the church the individual believer is invited, not to listen to someone else pray, but to join in prayer with others. He does not come to watch someone else perform the acts and make the gestures of worship, but to worship.

The ORDINANCES

It has been a tradition for most of the Christian Church throughout its history that the observance of the sacraments is the Church's highest moment of worship. Baptists would not dissent from this opinion, though most of our people would object to the word *sacraments* and prefer instead the word *ordinances*.

By "ordinance," we stress the character of these rites performed by the Church in obedience to Christ's command; they are "ordained" by him for the Church's observance. This is indeed the first thing that distinguishes an ordinance in our Baptist churches from other ceremonies and practices which by tradition have acquired an honored place: the ordinance is commanded by Christ himself.

A second necessary element in setting off the ordinances from all other ceremonies is that they are to be proclamations of the gospel. That is, in the observance of the ordinances, the central message of the gospel ought to be expressed. This we believe we do in the observance of the two ordinances practiced by Baptist churches, baptism and the Lord's Supper. John Smyth, the early English Baptist, expressed it in this way: "That the sacraments have the same use that the word hath: that they are a visible word, and that they teach to the eye of them that understand as the word teacheth the ears of them that have ears to hear. . . ."[1] This is an echo of the idea of John Calvin that the sacraments are sacraments of the Word and that the proclamation of the Word must accompany them. More precisely, the Baptist view is that the ordinances are themselves a proclamation of the word of God.

A third requisite is that the ordinance must be an act of the Church. In this way it is distinguished from other commands of Christ, and other forms of proclaiming the gospel which may be primarily personal or individual. To participate in communion or to be baptized is not a private affair, but is rather to share in the declaration of the gospel of Christ, in obedience to his commands, within the church which he founded.

BAPTISM

It is from the ordinance of baptism that we have our name. Though the early English Baptists did not use the name, preferring to speak of themselves without a formal designation, their distinctive views on the subject of baptism soon led others to label them thus. What then began as a term of opprobrium soon became a gladly-accepted name, to be worn with honor and gratitude.

To non-Baptists, the most distinctive thing about our

---

[1] *From the* "Propositions and Conclusions concerning True Christian Religion, containing a Confession of Faith of certain English people, living at Amsterdam," *quoted by* Lumpkin, *op. cit.*, p. 138.

practice of the ordinance of baptism is our insistence upon immersion as the proper mode of observance. Other Christian denominations use this practice on occasion, of course. It was standard practice in the western church for centuries, as it still is in the eastern churches. Baptists have been more nearly unanimous in stressing the mode of immersion, however, as the proper way to continue the practice of primitive Christianity. Yet, even the English Baptists of the first generation did not use this form. The researches of William H. Whitsitt in the late nineteenth century showed beyond any reasonable doubt that the practice of immersion was re-established among English Baptists about 1640. Since that time it has come to be the accepted mode, and it is right today to connect the name and the mode.

We hold to the practice of immersion, not out of a desire to be contentious, but because we believe it to be most truly representative of the original intention of the ordinance. There is not only the general practice of the early church and of several centuries to sustain us in this insistence. The very word *baptize*, which has been transliterated into English, portrays an act of dipping or immersing. Baptists do not see any adequate grounds for exchanging what we believe to be a command of the Lord for something else which is at best a substitute for the original practice of the Church.

It is important, too, that baptism by immersion proclaims the gospel in a way not possible in the act of sprinkling or pouring. If, as we believe, a requisite for a church ordinance is that it be such a proclamation, then a change for the sake of convenience is not acceptable. The language of Paul in Romans 6 is clear on the meaning of baptism, and he connects the act with the Christian affirmation of the death, burial, and resurrection of Jesus. Baptism is a dramatic declaration of the central event of history for the Christian.

It is also a declaration of the personal commitment to Christ. Any public act of confession might seem to fulfil this requirement. Yet, Paul says that baptism offers this powerful symbolism: the believer is lowered into the water and is raised again to signify his death to an old way of life and his being brought forth to a new way. ". . . like as Christ was raised from the dead by the glory of the Father, even so you also should walk in newness of life" (Rom. 6:4). The message of the gospel is not complete, of course, in the description of past events. It includes the present meaning of those events in the lives of believers today, and this is proclaimed by the believer who confesses, in his baptism, the gift of new birth, new life, by God's mercy and grace.

Baptism is an eschatological ordinance, too. That is, it speaks of the Christian hope. Though all our religious words and deeds are symbols, and our efforts to go beyond symbolic expression must fail, baptism declares the hope of the Christian in the final resurrection, the triumph over death and its sting through the same power of God that saves us from the death which is sin.

Even more significant than the insistence upon immersion is our Baptist belief about the proper subject of baptism. Though the English churches were slow in coming to the practice of immersion, they had begun their distinctive existence with the demand that baptism be administered only to responsible persons who had affirmed their personal faith in Christ and their acceptance of his Lordship and of the discipline of the Church.

Our insistence is not based upon the recent discoveries of scholars, but upon the New Testament and what we find there clearly indicated concerning baptism and indeed the very nature of the gospel and its invitation. Our practice is not "adult" baptism as opposed to that of "infants," but rather that of baptizing only those who are capable of making, and have made, their own personal commitment to Christ in faith. Thus, we baptize children if we believe they have come to such a decision and response.

It will be obvious, therefore, that we do not regard baptism as a continuation of the practice of circumcision in Christian guise. To make such an identification would, of course, enhance the idea of continuity between Judaism and Christianity, but it would fit Christianity to a pattern which the New Testament has discarded. The new wine of the Christian gospel cannot be contained in the old wine-skins of Judaism's legal code or of birthright religion. The new message of the gospel included the call to faith, a faith that is intelligent and responsible. Thus do men enter the Church, which Baptists recognize as the company of those who are being saved by the power of God. It is not an ark of salvation, but the company of those who have responded to God's call in Jesus Christ.

Some readers will wonder about the absence of any mention of the covenant. There are denominations which justify the practice of infant baptism, not on the specific analogy of the rite of circumcision, but on the broader concept of the covenant. God made a covenant with Abraham, and by the terms of this covenant he and all his descendants were included in the promise of God's favor. And is not the New Testament a new covenant? Yes, but it does not follow that the terms of participation in the new one are identical with those of the old. Indeed, it is difficult to escape the repeated and insistent New Testament challenge to faith, as contrasted with an appeal to birthright, as the basis of this new covenant.

"But," some will say, "do you then leave unattended those who die in infancy, before they can reach the age of responsible personal faith? Would a merciful God allow these to be lost through no fault of their own, with no opportunity to exercise saving faith?" No, Baptists do not say this. There are some Baptists, as there are some in other denominations, who are extreme predestinarians, even to the point of fatalism. These believe that by eternal and unchangeable decrees God has willed that some should be saved and others lost, and any human efforts are unavailing to change one's prospects. But Baptists in general do not subscribe to this view. Neither do we hold that man is condemned for the stain of an inherited sin, nor that baptism is designed to wash away such a stain. On the other hand, we do believe that God's mercy, which is extended to us without any merit on our part, is equally rich and sufficient for those who have no power of choice or opportunity for faith.

Is baptism then not a means of grace? There is divided opinion among our people on this question. Generally, our response has been that it is not. We have tended to stress the nature of baptism as an act of obedience and witness on the part of the Christian, and have neglected any consideration of it as an event in which God acts. This attitude on our part has not been accidental or unthinking. It has been prompted by a desire to avoid a superstitious view of the ordinance which would treat it as having magical efficacy. In America, it has been strengthened by the controversy in the early nineteenth century with the followers of Alexander Campbell. Campbell, who was for a time a Baptist, taught a doctrine of baptismal regeneration. While commendably stressing the importance of the rite, his view seemed to make the physical act of baptism the central thing in the Christian experience. In his attempts at "reform," he led many Baptist churches and even entire associations to adopt this view and to make it a test of fellowship. In the separation that followed, those churches that remained Baptist tended to lean even further away from any stress upon the divine activity in baptism.

The renewed interest in baptism throughout the Christian community has prompted many Baptist theologians to take another look at our traditional teaching. British Baptists, as a rule, speak more clearly to this point than do we in America. Today there is a growing acknowledgment that, even on the basis of our description of baptism as an act of obedience, some room must be made for the act of God. We do not exclude Him from any realm of life. He is present in the moment of conversion, and even faith itself is possible only as His gift and as response to His call. Surely He does not then step aside to let baptism, done in obedience to His command, be a purely human act. It is, though not a magical or mechanical dispensation of salvation, surely a means of grace given to the believer.

THE LORD'S SUPPER

Like baptism, the Lord's Supper partakes of the three essential qualities which Baptists believe to belong to the ordinances. It is done in obedience to the command of Christ, it is a proclamation of the central truth of the gospel, and it is an act of the Church rather than a merely personal act. The name which we use here is the most common designation among Baptists, partly because it stresses the divine command. The words "This do in remembrance of me" are quoted or read in every Baptist observance of the Supper. Stress is laid upon this aspect of the ordinance in sermons devoted to the theme. Again, the words quoted above emphasize the Supper as a preaching of the gospel. It exhibits in dramatic fashion the belief that the death of Jesus was not just another death, nor just another instance of grave injustice done to a good man. We believe indeed that He died for others, that His death declares, demonstrates and offers God's redemptive love to man. We believe that in a vital sense His followers participate in His sacrifice and in new life through Him. All this is declared in the Supper. Further, we believe that His command to re-enact the scene of the Last Supper is a direction to the Church, His servant and messenger.

Of special interest is the interpretation of the Lord's

Supper held by the Baptists. It would be expected that our people would reject the view of the Roman Catholic Church, represented by the word "transubstantiation." This view, that the substances of the bread and wine are transformed so they actually become the body and the blood of the Lord, though the "accidents," or externals remain the same, is not acceptable to us. We do not see the need of it, nor do we find it in the New Testament. Almost equally unacceptable is the Lutheran view of "consubstantiation." Here more emphasis is put upon the reception of the sacrament in faith, and this, of course, we endorse. Yet, the view itself fails to satisfy us for the same reasons as above.

A third general interpretation is that ascribed to John Calvin, the Genevan reformer, who argued for a doctrine of the real presence of Christ in the Supper, but insisted that it was a spiritual rather than a bodily presence. Thus, in his view, the elements were not transformed, either by action of the priest or by the believing participation of the communicant. Yet, the faithful "truly partake of Christ, and feed on him."

A fourth way of interpreting the Supper is ascribed to Ulrich Zwingli, the Swiss reformer at Zurich, though the correctness of this ascription is contested by some Zwingli scholars today. It restricts the meaning of the ordinance to that of a memorial meal, in which the Christians commemorate the sacrificial death of Christ by a solemn observance. It is commonly said that this is the Baptist view of the Supper.

There is some foundation for attributing this view to us, and it is likely that a majority of Baptist pastors stress this interpretation whenever they preach on the subject. However, it is not correct to name this as "*the* Baptist view," since there are many Baptists who hold to a larger interpretation, one nearer to that of Calvin. And there are strong traditional reasons for doing so. In the Second London Confession of 1677, Chapter XXX treats of the Lord's Supper at some length. The second paragraph of that chapter seems to affirm the Zwinglian interpretation:

> In this ordinance Christ is not offered up to his Father, nor any real sacrifice made at all, for remission of sin of the quick or dead; but only a memorial of that one offering up of himself, by himself, upon the crosse, once for all; and a spiritual oblation of all possible praise unto God for the same. . . .[2]

In the seventh paragraph of the same chapter a fuller statement of meaning is offered, and this definitely goes beyond the former:

> Worthy receivers, outwardly partaking of the visible Elements in this Ordinance, do then also inwardly by faith, really and indeed, yet not carnally, and corporally, but spiritually receive and feed upon Christ crucified & all the benefits of his death; the Body and Blood of Christ, being then not corporally, or carnally, but spiritually present to the faith of Believers, in that Ordinance, as the Elements themselves are to their outward senses.[3]

It will be seen from this account that there is not a distinctive Baptist doctrine of the Lord's Supper. There is no special Baptist viewpoint as to the practice of the ordinance or as to its meaning to set this way apart from the usages and views of other Christians. This is reflected in the relatively small amount of controversial literature published by the Baptists on this subject, as contrasted with an enormous amount on the topic of baptism. Yet, it ought to be said that this does not imply an indifference to the subject. Baptists can be just as contentious about their views on the Supper as on any other topic. Nevertheless, we have rightly sensed the issues here, while important and worthy of our careful study, are not of the kind that separate Christians

[2] *Quoted* in Lumpkin, *op. cit.*, pp. 292 f.
[3] *Ibid.*, p. 293.

into various denominations. They cut across the denominational lines.

Even on the manner of observing the Supper, and on its interpretation, we disagree among ourselves. Some of our churches restrict participation to the membership of the local congregation, and others insist that only Baptists ought to partake of the Supper in a Baptist church. Up to the middle of the nineteenth century, it was quite common for a Baptist association or convention to include in its program a place for the observance of the ordinance. Today many of our people would contend that this is improper, and that it ought to be celebrated only as the act of a congregation which is subject to a common discipline. The disagreement itself is a witness to the vitality with which the Baptist understanding of the Lord's Supper is endowed. It remains true, however, that these differences of opinion on this question are chiefly concerned with the administration of the ordinance. They do not distinguish us, as Baptists, from the general understanding of its significance in the life of the Church.

Our position with respect to baptism is different, for it is more than a question about the proper manner to observe a ceremony. The crucial issues in the doctrine of baptism are, after all, issues that concern the nature of the Christian Church. If the Church is to be composed of all the people of a nation, into which they are born and for which they need not make a personal commitment, then our doctrine of baptism is wholly wrong, and we ought to admit it. If, on the other hand, the Church is to be the company of those who in faith have surrendered their lives to God in Christ Jesus, those who have entered upon a pilgrimage as servants of God, then we cannot yield our position about the meaning of baptism, nor that about its form which is so closely bound up with its meaning.

CHRISTIAN ETHICS

Does Christ care for refugees?" asked a speaker in the 1955 meeting of the Baptist World Alliance. When he answered his own question in the affirmative, he was actually answering a much broader question as well. Does the Christian experience have an effect upon the attitude of man to fellow man? Does the Christian gospel have implications for the daily conduct and the personal standards of life for the believer? Does the "Christian way" involve human relationships and responsibilities as well as one's relationship and responsibility to Almighty God? To all of these we answer "Yes."

This is not a Baptist answer, but a Christian one. There are those who still say that "ministers should simply preach the gospel, churches should stick to religion, and both should leave politics, social affairs, and economic matters alone." Happily this attitude is disappearing, and there is no serious interpreter of the Christian faith today who would draw a line of absolute division between the realm of religion and the concerns of daily life and work. Papal pronouncements on the obligations of doctors or on the rights of laboring men declare the unity of life and faith. Commissions and committees of the evangelical churches study the moral implications of wealth, marriage, and parenthood, of political power, and of the complexities of our modern society.

There is no clearly defined moral code which is a means of distinguishing Baptists from other Christians. We are a diverse people, and we count in our company some who are rigorists in some matters and others who exhibit a broadly tolerant attitude on the same questions. The views of our people are colored by political and social systems, as well as by other elements in our culture. We tend to reflect the moral standards of our setting, as indeed all people do. Our prohibitions and exhortations are frequently more of a testimony to these environmental factors than an explication of Biblical or theological truth, applied to human life.

The story is told about a young preacher in a Kentucky community who tried to make his first sermon memorable. He preached a fiery denunciation of horse racing. After the sermon one of his deacons took him aside and gently told him that this was a neighborhood noted for fine horses, and that many of the members of the church enjoyed the races. He took the hint, and for his next sermon turned his attention to tobacco, which he denounced with equal fervor. The same deacon later pointed out that the farmers in the area grew tobacco, and that his salary was paid, at least in part, by the gifts of these farmers. Not yet daunted, he next preached on the evils of drinking whiskey, only to be reminded that the church was in the shadow of distilleries and some of the church members worked there. He asked the deacon what he was to do, what he could denounce. The deacon replied, "Why not preach ag'in' them heathen witch doctors? There ain't one in a thousand miles of here!"

It is still possible to hear the evils of the city denounced in country churches, and the sins of the South in northern churches. It is easy to see the faults of others. More often, we hear our ministers describe the code of Christian conduct that expresses a provincial interest or awareness. In the 1940's a Baptist state convention vigorously denounced the use of tobacco, but said nothing about the Nazi oppression then rampant, nor even about the racial injustices being practiced within hearing distance of their meetingplace. Again, another state convention has spoken and acted much more emphatically about dances held on the campus of a denominational college than about racial discrimination.

This problem is not new. One may read in our journals of a century ago of the moral problems which beset our people. The editors would devote pages to answering such a query as "Is it right for Christian people to attend concerts?" At the same time, unchecked evils in our economic system, which are now quite obvious to us, were going unnoticed by both editors and inquirers.

A generation ago a mountain preacher was approached by a hearer whose reputation for occasional drunkenness, rowdiness and moonshining was quite well-established. "Preacher," he said, "don't the Scripture say something about 'Love not the world, nor the things of the world'?" The preacher answered, "Yes, I believe it does say something like that." The inquirer came back with "Well, preacher, if that don't mean Sunday baseball, what *does* it mean?"

Well, what does it mean? What are the areas of moral concern for the professing Christian? What are the ethical issues on which the Church should speak and act, as a consequence of Christian discipleship?

No satisfactory ethical theory will arbitrarily divide these issues into personal and public responsibilities. It is not possible to put upon any group the responsibility for choices that must, in the last analysis, be personal.

MATTERS OF PERSONAL CHOICE
AND CONDUCT

Moral issues are most clearly seen in areas where personal decision must be exercised. At such points the greatest diversity is likely to be manifest. Here, too, the dangers of legalism are greatest. Equivocation is not so easy for the individual as for the group; hence specific answers are called for, graded in terms of acceptability, and finally approved or disapproved as possible or impossible for the Christian, as a Christian, to maintain. Once such a standard is generally adopted, another short step may lead to the expectation that it will be upheld by legal sanctions and regulations. Even where the help of the government in enforcement is not sought, the discipline of the Church may be invoked, and the weight of the general approval or disapproval of the congregation employed to implement the consensus of moral judgment.

One of these areas of great concern today is the use of alcoholic beverages. Baptists have not always spoken unanimously against such use, nor have they agreed on the manner of implementing their convictions. There is probably less agreement on these questions today than ever before. In the early nineteenth century, when many churches still paid their pastors' salaries "in kind," some pledged not only so many gallons of molasses, so many bushels of potatoes, and a certain amount of meat, but also so many gallons of corn whiskey as salary. Even then, however, drunkenness was frowned upon, and a member might be excluded from the fellowship of a Baptist church for overindulgence. Temperance societies were already in vogue, both in England and in America, and a proportionate part of their membership and support apparently was drawn from among the Baptists.

Toward the end of the nineteenth century, total abstinence had won its way as the Christian ideal among our people, and preachers were almost unanimous in denouncing drinking as a vice and a sin. Baptists were influential in getting local prohibition laws and in the passage of the Eighteenth Amendment to the Constitution.

It has been suggested that the swing to the extreme, not only of personal abstinence but of governmental prohibition, was conditioned by our frontier experience. It is interesting that the two great camp-meeting groups, the Methodists and the Baptists, have been the prominent advocates of prohibition. Perhaps our institutional interests in this connection produced an emotional attitude on the subject of liquor. Liquor consumption resulted in rowdiness and the frequent disruption of camp-meeting and brush arbor services. Such disturbances created an understandable hostility, beginning with the ministers and easily transmitted to the faithful. What was more natural than to strike at what appeared to be the root of the trouble?

The attitude of Baptists today on this question is clearly modified from that of absolute prohibition. While ministers still speak with almost a single voice in favor of abstinence, our laymen are clearly divided, and the practice of disciplining a member for drinking is much less common than a generation ago. We have had to leave to the judgment of the electorate the question of the wisdom or folly of Federal or state prohibition. We were deprived of some of our strongest moral arguments by the corruption of officialdom during prohibition days, resulting from the illegal traffic in liquor. Our acquaintance with Baptist and other Christian brethren in other places, for whom the problem has never appeared so acute, may have helped to create a milder and less rigid attitude among our people.

We are clearly faced with difficult problems of regulation in a complex society. The retreat from a policy of advocating governmental prohibition does not express any lessening of concern with the basic problems; it may, indeed, declare that the churches are ready to re-assume responsibility for guidance on matters which have moral meaning for their people, instead of relying on the forces of the state.

In the matter of gambling, our Baptist people have shown more unanimity. Though our profession and our practice are not fully identical, we have spoken with equal vigor against the evils of gambling, whether in the form of betting on horse races or dog races in Arkansas, lotteries in Louisiana, or casino gambling in the resort centers. A recent statement of the American Baptist Convention, in the form of a resolution adopted by the delegates to the 1959 meeting, says it well:

We are opposed to gambling in all its forms because:

Gambling is essentially the redistribution of a people's wealth according to chance, rather than according to the receiver's contribution to society;

The presence of widespread gambling is a symptom of economic decay and an indication that industrious, thrifty and responsible living have failed, and people in their despair are throwing away what they have today on the chance that it might bring returns tomorrow.

When a government "legalizes" gambling for the sake of adding to its revenue under the pretext of easing the tax burden it participates in a mass swindle in that it sets up a system whereby its people are induced to part with a far larger total sum of money, from which only a fraction replaces taxes and the government becomes a partner in deceit.[1]

Our society in general has not advanced as far in understanding the compulsive gambler as in understanding the alcoholic. Surely, such a better understanding ought to be sought, and it may be that our Baptist fellowship can pioneer in this effort. We need not soften our opposition to the evil effects of gambling in the effort to deal sympathetically with

[1] *Yearbook of the American Baptist Convention, 1959* (New York: American Baptist Convention, 1959), p. 165.

its victims. At any rate, we are now showing some evidence of a clearer understanding of what is involved in the problem. A generation ago many of our pronouncements on the subject were subsumed under a discussion of amusements, and there was an easy identification of gambling with any game played with cards, the "devil's pasteboards." Expressions on this topic in recent years reflect three significant changes in Baptist sentiments. We recognize that it is not a matter of purely private morals, but a general social concern; that insofar as it is of private concern, it is not a matter for nit-picking legislation but for the development of a sense of moral responsibility; that public policy on gambling must have a basis in the total life of the people, including the public welfare, rather than in the restricted moral code of a small segment of the public.

The question of proper amusements for the Christian has always been a matter of great concern. Early in the twentieth century one could hear sermons in most of our churches on themes of this kind, though the particular amusement subjected to criticism, denunciation, or prohibition would, of course, vary according to the convictions of the preacher and the general cultural pattern of acceptance or rejection in the area. Some were critical of card-playing in any form. Others regularly denounced the theater, or "joy riding" on Sunday, or dancing. A little later, the movies came in for their share of criticism.

Within the past decade, one might even hear sermons devoted to the evils of television. Much of this criticism, however, seems to stem from the idea that this entertainment offers strong competition to the church services, particularly on Sunday evenings. The fact that this medium of communication and entertainment has appeared only in recent years is, no doubt, responsible for our saner attitude toward it than towards some other forms. We are meeting the challenges and opportunities which it offers in a more mature way, corresponding to the maturity which we are achieving in other realms. Some of our Baptist agencies are producing some informative and wholesome television programs that are both technically well-done and religiously significant.

As far as official pronouncements and sermons are concerned, Baptists are still united in their views of Sunday observance. The so-called Puritan view of the "Christian Sabbath" is ours by tradition. Sunday is a day for rest and worship, and the labors of the week are to be put aside, "works of mercy and necessity only excepted." Yet, in this area, too, the complexity of our modern society compels us to recognize the impossibility of an absolute standard. The frontier conditions, in which all activity of the community save that of the church might come to a halt for a full day, are no longer with us. The legalist who refuses to buy a newspaper on Sunday may feel no compunction in buying one which was printed on Sunday. He may buy a bottle of milk early Monday morning only because others worked on Sunday to have that milk at the supermarket ready for him. We cannot take shelter in a structure of our own private actions, because we live in an interdependent society.

State and local laws regulating or prohibiting business activities on Sunday are currently being challenged in many court actions. We must keep in mind our convictions concerning religious liberty, and we must be careful not to impose our religious convictions upon others by force of law. Robert Robinson, an English Baptist preacher of the eighteenth century, put it thus in *Reflections on Liberty of Conscience*:

> Another part of Christianity consists of duties to be performed. Liberty to be a practical Christian is liberty to perform these duties, either as they regard God, our neighbor, or ourselves. Liberty to be a Christian implies liberty not to be a Christian, as liberty to examine a proposition implies liberty to reject the arguments brought to support it, if they appear

inconclusive, as well as liberty to admit them, if they appear demonstrative.

MATTERS OF SOCIAL RESPONSIBILITY

It is a part of Christian morality to recognize that "no man is an ilande unto himselfe." Our actions, even those which we judge to be of a private and personal sort, have implications which almost always affect our fellow men. Yet, there are some of the areas of moral concern which are more clearly important for human relationships than others. In 1914, the Social Service Commission of the Southern Baptist Convention made its first report to the convention. It indicated the scope of its concern thus: "The manifold social task of the modern Church is the same as that of the early Church, namely, the task of realizing the will of God in all human life." That part of human life which immediately and necessarily involves a relationship between two people, or among several, calls for additional consideration.

The same commission report mentioned above addressed itself directly to some of the most urgent problems of the day: "Upon business the Church must impose its ennobling restraints. It must check private greed and compose class antagonisms. It must . . . insist . . . that the workers have a fair share in the prosperity which they produce." The following year the perspective was broadened, and the commission spoke sharply about "social inequality . . . industrial injustice . . . bad housing . . . crowded tenements . . . heartless greed in corporate wealth . . . graft in politics . . ." and other ills.

As Christians in the latter half of the twentieth century, we may be distressed over the apparent blindness of our fathers to some moral problems. Yet, even the readiness to consider the matters mentioned above represented quite an advance. In the first place, we must still struggle against an age-old lingering feeling that the Christian is not to be involved in the affairs of an evil world, and that the church should maintain a lofty disdain toward questions of an economic, political, or social nature. One aspect of this attitude is shown in the tension within the early Church, when there was a strong insistence that the Christian could not "bear the sword" as soldier or magistrate, or otherwise serve the imperial government. Our early English Baptist ancestors had to wrestle with the same question. Some of their number were drawn to the view of certain continental Anabaptists, who clearly forbade those of their company to hold public office. After considerable discussion, the Baptists took the position that "it is lawful for a Christian to be a magistrate or civil officer," and we have maintained this belief in the succeeding generations. Yet, this has not dispelled the lingering notion that the action of the Christian in the political realm is set in a compartment of his life separated from his Christian profession.

A related attitude is found, in the second place, in the idea that the gospel is concerned only with spiritual matters, or only with the hereafter. Thus, any attempt of the church to speak to the social and economic issues of the day is a matter of meddling. In 1888, a resolution on temperance was presented to the Southern Baptist Convention. The president, James P. Boyce, ruled it out of order because it was "not germane to the work of the convention." Unfortunately, one still hears, in Baptist circles as well as elsewhere, the insistence that "the preachers ought just to preach the gospel and quit meddling in other things" like race relations, labor-management relations, business practices, and politics.

That we had come so far by the early part of this century that we could begin to speak with a single voice on such issues is due, in part, to our coming of age. There are signs in other areas that by this time the Baptist fellowship had achieved a self-awareness as an influential voice in public affairs, and with this came a sense of responsibility to the rest of the Christian world and to the public at large. At the same time, it is difficult for a large company of people, as diverse as we Baptists are, to be prophetic in interpreting the needs and issues of the times. We were (and are) growing very fast, and our prosperity in membership and in wealth has perhaps encouraged a conservative attitude on social questions as well as in other areas. We need the prayers of the Christian world that we shall not let our sense of mission be swallowed up in our sense of self-esteem. The transition from austerity to prosperity is never easy. And how can one learn in advance the responsibilities that belong to maturity?

The great prophet of social righteousness, Walter Rauschenbusch, was a Baptist. To him, we and other American Protestants owe a debt of immeasurable proportions for calling our attention to some of our responsibilities to our fellow man. His *Christianity and the Social Crisis* and *Christianizing the Social Order* are classics in the field of social ethics. Some of the ideas which he advanced were revolutionary in his day, but are now almost universally acknowledged by our people. Though the "social gospel" was roundly attacked by those who feared it de-emphasized personal religious experience, the personal piety of Rauschenbusch himself was beyond question. As recently as the 1930's one might hear polemical sermons from Baptist pulpits denouncing the social gospel, though many of these were in reality aimed at a parody or an exaggeration of the views of Rauschenbusch. Today such sermons are a thing of the past.

During World War I a moral issue of the most pressing kind was brought to the attention of the world Christian community. Baptists, along with others, took note of the fundamental questions of war and peace, of the reported atrocities, and of the increased demand for social services to the military, to war widows and orphans, and to war-ravaged communities. Many of our ministers "presented arms" and preached the righteousness of the war to make the world safe for democracy. Not until the post-war years did we give gen-

eral support to the cause of disarmament and the renuncia-
tion of war as an instrument of national policy. Not all the
lessons of World War I were forgotten in the war of 1939-
1945. Happily, the bonds of Christian brotherhood were able
to survive the bitterness of war. Gestures of concern were ex-
changed through neutral countries during the war, and at the
end of hostilities old ties of fellowship were renewed and
strengthened. A German Baptist tells of the first Scandinavian
Baptists to visit Germany after the war, and how they brought
food and clothing to share with the defeated people.

In general, the English Baptists have been in advance of
their American brethren in social consciousness. In the eighteenth century, John Howard was influential in the prison reform movement. Baptists there were active also in seeking to
abolish the slave trade, and a generation before our American
Civil War they were urging their American brethren to join
them in seeking the freedom of the slaves. Others energetically
pushed for more truly representative Parliaments, for general
suffrage, and for the repeal of acts that discriminated against
dissenters from the established church.

In twentieth century America, one of the most crucial
areas of ethical concern is that of marriage and the family. The
rapid increase in the divorce rate and other evidences of
marital failure have brought this problem to the center of
interest, not only for Baptists but for all Christian denominations.

Baptists take seriously the Biblical words concerning
marriage and divorce. The discipline of our churches is not
uniform, however, and the strictness with which these Biblical
injunctions are applied is dependent upon our understanding
of the Bible as a whole. In those churches where the Bible is
regarded as a book of laws, a more rigid interpretation of the
words of Jesus and the apostles is manifest than in others.

The most common position of our people is that divorce
is permissible only on "Scriptural grounds"—that is, that the

"innocent party" may sue for divorce on the grounds of marital infidelity. In most cases this "innocent party" is considered free to remarry without stigma or blame. Some congregations would, however, withdraw fellowship from a member who remarries after a divorce, for whatever cause, so long as the former spouse is still living. Many other churches would not elect such a person to a church office.

In recent years our increased awareness of the problems of marriage and the home has produced some constructive efforts. With the aid of theological and sociological insights, we are coming to see the possibility of establishing our homes upon a stronger foundation than that of transient affection or mere infatuation. We recognize, too, that divorce is a symptom of a failure that has preceded the legal proceedings, and that there are many broken homes that are not publicized through the legal dissolution of the marriage bond. Premarital counseling is one of the most important duties of the minister, and many of our theological schools have recognized this in the introduction of training in this field for the young ministers. Family life conference for teachers, pastors, and counselors are offering aid in diagnosis and treatment of some of the ills of our homes. Publications like *Home Life*, published by the Southern Baptist Convention, offer informative and inspirational literature intended to strengthen the homes of our members. Not all of the conditions that threaten the stability of marriage and the home can be met and altered through such means, but the appearance of these efforts is a hopeful sign.

The consideration of the foregoing matters of ethical import allows us again to raise the question, "Do Baptists participate in the life of the world at large?" We are glad to say that we do. Through the offices of the Baptist World Alliance, as well as through relief committees established by various other Baptist groups, we have been ministering to refugees and displaced persons since the end of World War II. That we are active in the area of political responsibility is evident at every level of government. Some of our people are active today in responsible positions in the Peace Corps, in the State Department, and in various other executive offices. Baptists serve in the Congress and on the Supreme Court of the United States. In other nations, too, our people are active in the affairs of state and society. The vice-president of Liberia, the Honorable William Tolbert, is a Baptist who serves as a pastor in addition to his governmental duties. In terms of participation, then, and in terms of our concern with vital issues, Baptists have a contribution to make to the moral decisions of our time.

If this is true, what do Baptists have to say about that most crucial area for Christian ethics today, the relations between people of different races?

RACE RELATIONS

So urgent a matter as this deserves specific and separate treatment. It involves personal conduct, and at the same time it is a matter for public policy. In the United States today it is particularly crucial, most of all in the southern states. Here, Baptists are more numerous than anywhere else, and we even represent a majority of the total church membership in many southern communities. Consequently, we bear a large part of the responsibility for the current state of race relations, in proportion to our leadership potential in the various communities.

It is still true, as so many have remarked, that the 11 o'clock hour on Sunday morning is the most segregated time of the week in America. It is also true that many in our Baptist churches, as well as in others, do not see in this fact anything inconsistent with the professions of belief in Christian brotherhood or with the meaning of the gospel.

English Baptists were generally earlier in their recognition of a profound moral question in race relations than were

American Baptists. As early as 1830 they were urging their American brethren to join them in a crusade to put an end to the slave trade and to free all the slaves. The American Triennial Convention of Baptists politely refused to take any action, on the grounds that the convention did not have authority over the churches sharing in its work. Even at this time, however, there were some influential American Baptists who shared these abolitionist sentiments.

By 1844 the anti-slavery conviction had grown so that, when a test case was made, the Triennial Convention refused to approve the appointment of a slaveholder. The statement of the Foreign Mission Board was clear:

> If . . . anyone should offer himself as a missionary, having slaves, and should insist on retaining them as his property, we could not appoint him. One thing is certain, we can never be a party to any arrangement which would imply approbation of slavery.

As a result of this decision, various Southern state conventions and auxiliary mission societies withdrew, and the next year the Southern Baptist Convention was formed. In a sense, the Baptists of the North had delivered their souls with respect to the question at hand, though of course they had not come to grips at all with the further issues of race relations which are today of paramount importance.

In the pre-Civil War days, even in the slaveholding South, it was the usual thing for slaves to be members of the same church with their masters. This was a relationship characterized by a paternal, rather than a fraternal attitude on the part of the white people. In those cases where Negroes had their own church services, it was a standard requirement that a white man must be present for each meeting—apparently to guard against the possibility of the use of church meetings as an opportunity to plot insurrections. Although soon after the war the practice arose of forming separate congregations for the Negroes—in some cases, at least, as much from their own initiative as from that of the whites—this practice did not receive universal approval. Many of the churches of the Southern Baptist Convention numbered Negroes in their membership even after 1900.

In general, the pattern of church membership in the latter one-third of the last century and the first half of the present century has been one of segregation. Negro Baptists have formed their own local, state, and national organizations.

Some "white" churches have been open to Negro membership throughout the past century, and the number is increasing. Although up to this time there are few Southern Baptist Churches that have Negro members, in 1961 the American Baptist Convention reported that almost one-third of its churches were racially inclusive. The position of that convention was made clear in a resolution adopted in 1959:

> As American Baptist Christians and followers of our Lord and Savior Jesus Christ, we . . . vow that we will work in whatever ways are open to us in the place where we live and in our land to break down the barriers that exist between us and persons of different racial and national origins.
>
> . . . we do agree: that members of our churches should base their fellowship and associations on individual merit without regard to national origins.

At the level of cooperative work, such as that of the conventions, the policies of segregation are disappearing even more rapidly. In addition to the churches of the American Baptist Convention that are racially inclusive, there are many churches made up wholly of Negro members who share in the life and work of the Convention, some of them dually aligned, thus keeping their ties with the national organizations of Negro Baptists.

Such comparisons as the one just made will be indicative of the more conservative attitude of Southern Baptists, and, of course, they reflect the difficulty with which deep-rooted traditions and prejudices are changed. Yet, even in the South some progress is being made. In 1947 the Southern Baptist Convention made a significant stride forward in the approval of a report on race relations.

> Our responsibility is the more pressing because the problem of race relations is primarily a moral and religious problem. Political action, even at its best, cannot do what must be done. Laws create a measure of restraint against injustice and mark out certain procedures under the sanction of governmental power. But we are seeing the truth today that law, even the Constitution of our Nation, cannot relax tensions and resentments, nor banish the prejudices and injustices that spring from fallacious thinking and racial feeling. These things require the strong inward grip of religious faith and the inward demand of moral understanding and conviction. . . .
>
> And we Baptists, living in the midst of these tensions, must accept our responsibility. We cannot dismiss the problems of race relations as a side issue. We must be willing to shoulder the difficult and continuing task.

This declaration prepared the way for the convention's action in 1954, when the meeting was held soon after the historic decision of the United States Supreme Court concerning segregation of the public schools.

> In the light of the recent decision handed down by the Supreme Court of our nation declaring segregation of the races to be unconstitutional, and in view of the position of this Convention in adhering to the basic moral principles of our religion as they apply in race relations, we recommend:
>
> 1. That we recognize the fact that this Supreme Court decision is in harmony with the constitutional guarantee of equal freedom to all citizens, and with the Christian principles of equal justice and love for all men.
>
> 5. That we urge Christian statesmen and leaders in our churches to use their leadership in positive thought and plan-

ning to the end that this crisis in our national history shall not be made the occasion for new and bitter prejudices, but a movement toward a united nation embodying and proclaiming a democracy that will commend freedom to all peoples.

One more significant statement may be cited to indicate the level at which our Baptist conscience is functioning in this most difficult and demanding area of moral responsibility. It is found in a resolution adopted by the Baptist World Alliance Congress, meeting in Rio de Janeiro in 1960:

> We call, therefore, upon our Baptist people around the world to live above race prejudice and to take the lead in abolishing racial discrimination and removing the indignities of racial segregation and the caste system wherever these still exist.[2]

It must be remembered, of course, that the implementation of such a statement is far more difficult than its adoption. We cannot claim to have fulfilled this ideal in more than a token fashion.

We are advancing slowly; but we *are* advancing. All of the seminaries of the American Baptist Convention and the Southern Baptist Convention are open to qualified students regardless of race. Baptist colleges in several of the Southern states have opened their doors to Negroes. Local churches here and there, one by one, are removing racial barriers. In some places, where the barriers still stand, courageous ministers are speaking plainly and with genuine Christian compassion on the relevant issues. Some are paying the price of ostracism for their convictions, and even as these words are being written some Southern Baptist ministers are being forced out of their pulpits by unyielding bitterness and resistance to the proclamation of a gospel of love. Baptists do, in truth, hold to the theological affirmations about God and

[2] *Baptist World Alliance: Tenth Baptist World Congress*, *op. cit.*, p. 300.

man which make possible a genuine spirit of brotherhood. And where religious truth and traditional practices conflict, we cannot afford to sacrifice the former to save the latter. By the grace of God, in whom we trust and to whom our lives are committed, we shall surely, if slowly, seek to realize the will of God for all of human life.

PART III
HOW BAPTISTS
DO THEIR WORK

INTRODUCTION

Exalted expressions of truth and keen insights are put to their most severe tests when their owners seek to apply them. In the Christian church they are applied in personal relationships and in the sharing of work. In this part we shall describe the ways in which Baptists have tried to apply their understanding of the Christian way of life within their fellowship and in the performance of the labors which they have undertaken.

Ideally, a church's government should do two things. First, it should clearly express the distinctive religious insights of the church. Secondly, it should provide the church with the organization for fulfilling its mission. In actuality, the structure of church government is likely to be a compromise. Complicating factors enter the picture and modify the original intentions. The temper of the times, prevailing political ideas and practices, personal inclinations of strong leaders—all these help to shape church polity. Their influences may be seen in every denomination of Christians. They are present among Baptists, in the local congregations and in the larger fellowship of the denomination as well.

We shall look first at some of the principles of organization which are traditional among our people. Then we shall consider the structure and work of the local congregations and of the larger fellowship of Baptists. After this we shall examine some of the agencies and means employed by the churches in fulfilling their shared obligations in Christian ministries. All of this will help to portray a significant and appealing part of the Baptist way of life.

PRINCIPLES OF ORGANIZATION AND ORDER

Discussions of church order are usually considered boring. People who will listen willingly to sermons or missionary addresses will leave the assembly or fidget restlessly when the gathering begins to consider questions of ecclesiastical structure and polity. This is quite understandable, since the discussion often dwells upon minute points, and little effort is usually made to connect the issues of the moment with the great principles that have brought the people into a common body and made them a community.

It is proper, then, to set forth our way of life as it is expressed in organization by describing first some of the principles upon which the structures are based. The following appear to have been decisive in the ordering of the affairs of Baptist churches.

1. Perhaps the principle which first comes to the mind of an outside observer is that of local congregational government. Baptists appeared in the context of English puritanism as it was distilled through the minds of advocates of congregationalism. In that context this meant an insistence upon

the freedom of the congregation to conduct its business without any interference from an external ecclesiastical authority.

The constitution or charter of almost every Baptist association or convention clearly disavows any control over the affairs of the congregations. The preamble to the constitution of the Baptist World Alliance says: ". . . this Alliance may in no way interfere with the independence of the churches." This "independence" is jealously guarded because Baptists still remember the grave oppression which their forefathers suffered under church authority which aimed at uniformity among the churches. We intend never to be a party to such oppression on our part.

We prize the freedom of the local congregation, but we recognize that this is not an unlimited freedom. Indeed, the word "autonomy," which has often been used to describe this local independence, is falling into disfavor, because it suggests an absolute and total freedom from restraint, a "self-rule." Baptists do not intend this. They join with all other Christians in recognizing Jesus Christ as Head of the Church. The ultimate authority for the Church is not its own will but the will of God as revealed in Jesus Christ. "Theonomy" rather than autonomy would be accepted by every Christian as the rule of the Church.

Our disagreement with others at this point concerns the interpretation and application of that will of God. Baptists believe that there is no sufficient reason for vesting the power of interpretation and enforcement in a larger ecclesiastical body than the local congregation, or in individual representatives of such a larger body. They believe also that there is no justification in the New Testament for a church body "lording it over" the local congregations. At the same time, they believe that the character of the gospel and the nature of the Church may best be fulfilled and expressed through a locally governed community of believers. But this is not autonomy.

The congregation is under divine rule, bound to the Scriptures, liberated from external control by men in order that it may more truly acknowledge its bondage to the purpose of God.

2. The second principle, that of interdependence, is the counterpart of the first. The assertion of freedom for a local church does not prohibit the formation of associations which are entered voluntarily for the sake of fellowship, mutual aid, and the performance of work which might exceed the resources of a single small congregation. Indeed, we confess that we need each other, and we share in the trials and triumphs one of another.

Early in the history of seventeenth century Baptists "connectionalism" began to play an important role. These "connections" or associations were expressions of the shared Christian experience and of mutual concern. Article XLVII of the London Confession of 1644 (Particular Baptist) says:

> And although the particular Congregations be distinct and severall Bodies, every one a compact and knit Citie in it selfe; yet are they all to walk by one and the same Rule, and by all meanes convenient to have the counsell and help one of another in all needful affaires of the Church, as members of one body in the common faith under Christ their onely head.

3. The third principle is also quite closely related to the first, this time from another side. This is the insistence upon religious liberty. In negative terms, it means the rejection of any form of establishment of any religion under legal forms, and the freedom of all religious from state control. That no religion should enjoy special legal favor, privilege, or support, but that all should have liberty and equal protection under the law—this is a principle upon which Baptists have built consistently. This means that one's membership in the Church is not simply one aspect, the religious aspect, of his citizenship in the State. In the Baptist view, a church that is coextensive

with the nation does not possess the necessary marks of a church, or at best not the marks of a well-ordered church.

4. A fourth principle is closely related to the third, and it is also relevant for the first. It may be called the principle of responsible membership. Baptists insist upon local management and ordering of the congregation's affairs, as opposed to external control through a hierarchy, because those who participate in such local government are people who have made their own responsible decision of Christian commitment and church membership, acknowledging this commitment in their baptism as believers.

It is not, then, simply a debate about the exact form of a ceremony that has made believers' baptism such an important part of Baptist practice. It is rather the question of the nature of the Church. Baptists answer the question "What is Christian baptism?" in terms of the proper subject. The matter of the proper mode is subordinate to this. They answer the question "What is the Church?" in terms of its membership. The matter of precise arrangement of the offices is subordinate to this. The two questions are essentially the same.

Only within this context can the Baptist insistence upon "democratic" government be understood or supported. This word, like the word "autonomy," can be twisted out of its proper meaning. Indeed, it suffers from just the same weakness as does "autonomy." It makes a valid point in what it denies —namely, that the church is rightly governed by an aristocracy or a hierarchy. It also rightly affirms the role of the whole congregation in deciding upon its course of action or its position on a specific question. But unless it is made clear that this word has limits, it may be supposed that we are claiming the right of the Church to make her own laws. Here again, what is intended is that the final and authoritative rule for the Church is the will of God. Baptists believe that no special insight into that will has been given to the clergy, as distinguished from the laity, and that the nature of the gospel rather suggests that "priesthood of believers" which opens up the divine will to every regenerate mind.

5. This leads us logically to the fifth principle, that of lay leadership. Here again we must distinguish between what is denied and what is affirmed.

It is not intended by Baptists that a ruling order of the clergy should be overthrown so that its place might be taken by a ruling order of nonclerical members of the church. This principle is rather another way of affirming the responsible membership of all. The person who is not yet capable of being a responsible member should not yet become a member of the church. Responsibility rests upon the whole church, rather than upon the ordained ministers alone. Those who are not called to be pastors may still offer to the church real leadership, by precept and example, and in the official duties assigned to them by the whole congregation.

In frontier days, many churches were given leadership by revered though untrained local laymen, in the absence of pastoral leadership. Sometimes they were instructed by "exhorting deacons," who would deliver the only sermons heard by a frontier congregation during the long intervals between visits from itinerant preachers. Taking as their text a verse of Scripture or a thought from some recent sermon or religious literature, these unordained prophets would press the claims of God upon the lives of their listeners in forceful, if unpolished, language. Such a man provides some of the most vivid memories of the early youth of one of the authors of this book. He was so much loved that churches other than his own often asked for his counsel in matters of disagreement. Almost a bishop without portfolio, he farmed, went to church, and exhorted the saints with equal diligence, and half a dozen churches in the western part of a county in a southern state would enroll him high on the list of saints if we Baptists should ever start the process of canonizing the worthy servants of God who have gone before us.

Women have shared in this work of leadership. Most Baptist groups still do not ordain women to the ministry, and the total number of ordained women among all Baptists is quite small. Nevertheless, they hold important posts in almost all our churches. They may serve as ministers of music and education or as directors of youth activities. In many churches they serve as deacons (or deaconesses—some churches make no distinction in the title). They are sent as messengers to the associations and conventions, and many are elected to serve as trustees for various agencies and institutions of these larger organizations. The American Baptist Convention has four times elected a woman as president. Mrs. Louise Paw of Burma is one of the vice-presidents of the Baptist World Alliance, and five other women serve with her as members of the Executive Committee of that group in the current 5-year term.

Although the Southern Baptist Convention has not yet elected a woman to the office of president, it has often chosen men other than pastors to serve in that capacity. The roster of its presidents includes college and university presidents, a judge, a member of Congress, two governors, a businessman, and several seminary presidents and professors. It is significant that there is no device to limit the participation of unordained members in the affairs of any Baptist body, so far as the authors know. On the other hand, there are many rules which, for one Baptist body or another, insure the participation of laymen in these affairs, by requiring at least a certain percentage of laymen as members of a board or committee or commission.

This principle of lay leadership has another facet that must be examined briefly. It is the fact that among Baptists there is no essential difference between clergy and laymen. The ordination of a man to the ministry is the church's recognition of a divine call to the work of that ministry, for which he has exhibited proper gifts and personal commitment. It does not place upon him an indelible mark, nor does it elevate him to a status above that of the "ordinary layman." The state may give to the ordained man special recognition (as, for example, the authority to perform marriages). Yet, within her own activities, the Church is not bound to observe the traditional lines as to what is the work of the pastor. A church may call upon others of its members to perform pastoral functions, to teach, to administer the ordinances, to lead in worship, and otherwise to do those things commonly considered the work of the minister alone.

6. The sixth principle governing the structure of Baptists' work is the observance of the New Testament pattern. It has been traditional among our people to place heavy stress upon this point. Most earlier Baptist interpreters of the New Testament believed that it offered a single uniform pattern of church government, locally independent, congregationally governed, served by two kinds of officers—the pastor and deacons. More recently, many have come to recognize that among the New Testament churches there was a considerable diversity.

> The necessity for interpreting the historical details is further complicated by the fact that evidently there was no single, consistent pattern of church life in the apostolic era. . . .
>
> There is language suggestive of episcopal and of presbyterial as well as of congregational practice in the church life of the earliest generation of believers.[1]

We believe that the Church's order is significantly related to her faith. This means that the government of the Church should not obstruct the expression of the faith but should rather facilitate that expression. It also means that, for a people who emphasize the New Testament authority for their faith, it is only natural to turn to the New Testament for guidance in matters of order as well.

[1] S. A. Newman, "The Ministry in the New Testament Churches," in *What is the Church?*, compiled and edited by Duke K. McCall (Nashville, Tennessee: Broadman Press, 1958), p. 47.

7. Even this agreement does not mean that we can ignore the questions arising out of different needs in circumstances altogether altered from those of the first century Church. This set of questions, indeed, constantly changing with the changing conditions, may be held responsible for the seventh principle of church order. It is the principle of versatility, or perhaps better, adaptability. Along with the insistence upon basic agreement with the New Testament, Baptists have held to (and practiced more often than expressed or admitted) a freedom to introduce new offices to meet the churches' needs and to call upon members to fill those posts of service.

Whenever the Christian church has encountered new situations which seemed to call for new ministries or for additions to the work of others, she has not hesitated to create those offices or to assign those jobs. The church in Rome in the early centuries had exorcists, acolytes, and readers. Modern churches have their ministers of music, Sunday School superintendents, and church visitors.

These examples show that the Church has been ready to meet the changed and changing needs of each new age. This response to new challenge is sometimes reluctant, sometimes late, sometimes not daring enough; but the principle is acknowledged, and it has been put into practice many times. The Baptist people have shared the principle, as we have shared the hesitation of our Christian brethren before new tasks. It has been our intention, however imperfectly achieved, to be open to such new needs, to meet them in ways that will not betray the gospel or essentially alter the nature of the Church and her mission in the world.

The LOCAL CONGREGATION

September the 22nd day, and in the year of our Lord according to the computation used in England 1701. We whose names are here recorded did unanimously agree and consent and gave up ourselves together, as a church to walk together in the fellowship of the God of our Lord Jesus Christ.[1]

In this fashion an early English Baptist congregation reported its formation. It reflects the Baptist understanding of the Church in terms of the local company of believers, knit together in a personal relationship, in common response to the grace of God and to his call which has come to each through encounter with Jesus Christ.

Such a strong emphasis upon the local congregation has created the impression that Baptists do not have a doctrine of the Church Universal, or even that we specifically disavow any such use of the word *church*. Yet, it is no necessary part of the

[1] As quoted in *The Baptist Times*, September 20, 1951, p. 12.

Baptist doctrine of the Church to limit the usage of the word in this fashion. An equally appropriate and ancient view among our people is that expressed in the Second London Confession of 1677, in Chapter XXVI:

> 1. The Catholick or universal church, which (with respect to internal work of the Spirit, and truth of grace) may be called invisible, consists of the whole number of the Elect, that have been, are, or shall be gathered into one, under Christ the head thereof; and is the spouse, the body, the fulness of him that filleth all in all.[2]

The quotation with which we began this chapter indicates the way in which Baptist churches generally are formed. This movement may originate within the local group, though perhaps more frequently now it is initiated by a nearby church. Indeed, the new work may begin as a mission of an older and well-established church. When it has gained enough strength and stability to project and support its program of work and worship, it is then "cut loose" from the control of the mother congregation and is formally constituted as a church. Such a step is taken upon the advice and with the assistance of other neighboring churches, whose participation is a kind of recognition of the new church as a sister congregation.

THE MINISTRY OF THE CHURCHES

In Baptist churches, two kinds of ministry are recognized as traditional and standard, that of the pastor and that of the deacons. In a larger sense, the ministry of the church is composed of the entire church, since every member who is truly a part of the church has a ministry to fulfil, whether that of preaching, of visiting the sick, of teaching, of comforting, or of sharing. Our recognition of these two groups that are to be found in most or all of our churches is based upon the New

[2] Lumpkin, *op. cit.*, p. 285.

Testament. In the book of Acts, the apostles called upon the Jerusalem church to select seven men who would take over the duties of distributing food and "waiting upon tables," so that they (the apostles) might give themselves to the ministry of the Word. This has been taken by most of our people as the first instance of the office of deacon, though the title is not there assigned to the seven. Again, in the Pastoral Epistles directions are given for the selection of those who are to serve as bishops and as deacons.

The office of deacon is not for us, as for some sister denominations, a preliminary stage of training and proving before one becomes a full-fledged minister. It is a full ministry in itself, though the deacons do not give their full time to its duties. An exception to this limitation is found in the German Baptist churches and some few others, where women may commit themselves vocationally to the service of the church in hospitals or schools, in the office and work of deaconesses.

In general, the church takes the initiative in naming men (and women) to the office of deacon. We do not require here, as we do in the case of those named as "ministers" (i.e., pastors, or preachers), a sense of divine call to a lifetime service. While in many churches the deacons are chosen for life, the practice of selecting them for a specific term of service, such as five years, is increasing in frequency.

The deacons often form an advisory council to work with the pastor in providing leadership for the church's total program of work and worship. It is traditional for them to assist the pastor in the administration of the Lord's Supper, and to be charged with the administration of the church's charitable work. The precise extent of the leadership exerted by the diaconate depends upon the strength of its membership and the dependence of the pastor upon its counsel, rather than upon any traditional definition of its role in a Baptist church.

We have regularly insisted that the Church has no human priesthood, apart from the priesthood of all believers. Consequently, we have maintained that the leadership of the pastor is one of office rather than one of status. The ordination of a man to the ministry does not endue him with a special character and does not set him apart from his fellow-Christians, nor does it place him in a line of succession from the apostles. It is, instead, a recognition on the part of the Church of a divine call to a particular ministry in the Church and of the gifts which he has manifested for the fulfilment of that call.

In earlier days, the chain of events leading to ordination might be begun by the Church. A member might be approached by others in the Church with the suggestion that he apply himself to study and exposition of the Scriptures and exhortation of the brethren, to see whether he possessed the necessary abilities for the ministry. Such a suggestion might be followed up by the Church's action in licensing, or "liberating," a man to exercise his gifts in a kind of probationary period, to be followed, if successful, by ordination. The judgment of the Church was taken so seriously that a man would feel obliged to make such a test, even though his preferences were against it.

Such a case, apparently, was that recorded in the minutes of the Wake Forest Baptist Church of Wake Forest, North Carolina, on November 20, 1836:

> Resolved, that in our estimation our brethren _____ _____ and _____ are called of God to preach the gospel of Christ and that it is the duty of this church [to] authorize them to preach the gospel wherever they may be called; and that the pastor be authorized to furnish them with an instrument of writing signed by him and the clerk which shall be considered a license.

Nowadays, however, the initiative is almost always taken by the individual, who approaches the Church with a request for licensing. It is always expected that he will do this in consequence of a divine call to the work of the ministry, but there is no standard definition as to what constitutes this call, or how it is experienced. For some it takes the form of an inward mystical experience, while others profess a less dramatic but no less real sense of divine leadership in the vocational choice. The ways of God in dealing with men are surely no less varied than are the ways of men themselves, and it is wise not to stipulate the manner in which God will make his will known. The responsibility of preaching the gospel is a grave one, and the man who undertakes it surely needs the assurance that this is the will of God for his life, in whatever form that assurance may be given to him.

Since neither the individual church nor the pastor is under an external ecclesiastical authority, a church that is seeking a pastor is free to approach whomever it will and to negotiate directly with him. Suggestions and recommendations, sometimes solicited by the church, may be received from its members and from outsiders, and a pulpit committee is usually named by the church to carry on preliminary negotiations and to sift the recommendations before consideration by the whole congregation. It may be of interest to note the way in which a church in England approached Samuel Medley in 1771 when he was being considered for the pastorate.

> As to the church here, that so earnestly desires a visit from you, modesty forbids them commending themselves; but hope you will find them a people, that have tasted that the Lord is gracious, sound in the commonly received doctrines of the faith, lovers of experimental religion, and desirous to walk in all the commandments and ordinances of the Lord blameless.

Mr. Medley paid them the desired visit, and minister and church were well-impressed with each other. Shortly thereafter another communication came from the church:

> . . . we do solemnly, in the fear of God, and with all our hearts, give you this public and united call, to come among us, statedly to preach the word of God to us: believing . . . that

it is the will of the great Head of the church, you should be employed in this part of his vineyard.

The relationship of church and pastor is not always instituted on such a lofty plane, to be sure. The church may be guilty of looking for a "hired man," and the minister may be guilty simply of seeking a "job." Yet this example reflects truly what is intended in our Baptist way of forming the relationship.

The function of the pastor in one of our local churches may vary, like that of the deacons, depending upon the abilities and interests of the man and the demands of the situation. His basic duties always include these of preaching, conducting public worship, providing spiritual leadership for the congregation, ministering to the sick, bereaved, and needy, and seeking out the unchurched who may be within reach of the church. He must find time for his own continuing study and devotional life amid the daily demands of the church. If he possesses abilities and training in pastoral counseling, he may spend a major part of his time dealing with problems of grief, doubt, marital difficulties, guilt, and fear. Denominational work may claim another large part of his energies.

Above all else, however, the Baptist pastor is still expected to be a preacher. The great tradition of Protestant preaching has been shaped by men of many Christian denominations, and Baptists have contributed to it as well as received from it. The sermon is the center of most of the services in Baptist churches, and the strength of our churches is usually directly related to the strength of the preaching which they have enjoyed. The names of Andrew Fuller, Robert Hall, Charles Haddon Spurgeon, Alexander Maclaren, F. B. Meyer, John Jasper, John A. Broadus, and Harry Emerson Fosdick represent the lively and continuing tradition of powerful preaching among our people. A member of the pulpit committee of a large and somewhat sophisticated congregation recently said to a seminary professor, "We want a preacher this time. Our last pastor was a good leader and counselor, and we are grateful for his work, but we sense the need of some timely and powerful preaching. Can you help us find a man who experiences a powerful gospel and preaches it with power?"

The manifold duties of the pastors in our churches have led in many churches to a multiple ministry. Associated with the pastor there may be a minister of education, whose primary responsibilities are in the Sunday School and the training program of the church; a minister of music; one or more church visitors; a minister to youth, and perhaps one or more mission pastors. The Christian church throughout its history has shown the ability to devise new means for meeting new challenges, and the free tradition of Baptists gives us unusually large liberty in offering a relevant ministry for our times.

THE MEETINGS IN OUR CHURCHES

In order clearly to present the way Baptists do their work, it may be helpful to outline the activities of a local church. In this respect, as in others already mentioned, it is difficult to describe, in the presence of such diversity, a "typical" situation. Without intending to suggest that this is the "norm," the authors may perhaps be forgiven for choosing to picture a pattern which they know best, in the context of the Southern Baptist Convention. The reader will recognize that variations on this pattern are numerous, even within this Convention, and wider variations will be found in other Baptist settings.

Services are held Sunday morning and Sunday evening in most of our churches. In many places the structure of the service is almost the same for both hours. If a difference is made, it likely will be in that the evening service is less formal, with more congregational participation, and with gospel songs rather than hymns being used. The sermon in the Sunday evening service is likely to be evangelistic, aimed directly at winning converts. If the Lord's Supper is to be observed, it will be incorporated in the morning service, while the ordinance of baptism is more likely to be administered in connection with an evening service.

Preceding the morning service is the Sunday School hour. Classes are provided for every age group. Infants and toddlers are cared for in a nursery during this hour and during the service as well. The Sunday School is intended specifically as an occasion for Bible study, and the curriculum for the older groups is planned to cover, over the course of several years, most of the Old and New Testaments. This enterprise is open, of course, to people who are not members of the church, and the enrollment in the Sunday School is likely to be larger than the total membership of the church.

Similarly, before the evening service, there is a Training Union hour. While others are not excluded, this program is designed specifically for the members of the church. It incorporates Bible study, but its range is wider than that of the Sunday School, and may include a study of communism, missionary strategy, race relations, the nature of the Church, Christian history, alcoholism, and problems in contemporary theology. As the name suggests, the purpose of this work is to offer training in church membership. Many of the leaders of our churches today began their development in Christian insight and activity in the Training Union of a few years ago.

Another service that has been established in most of our churches by long tradition is the midweek prayer service. At other times during the week the women of the church will be meeting as the Women's Missionary Society, the men in a Brotherhood meeting, the boys as Royal Ambassadors, and the girls as the Girls' Auxiliary, all in one way or another giving attention to the mission and task of the churches in today's world.

Small wonder that an exhausted Baptist, after a busy week of church activities, exclaimed, "It takes a strong constitution to be a good Baptist!"

Even though we may at times be in danger of burning up all our energy in attending meetings or pursuing countless activities related to these organizations, these all express a vitality and an intense concern that all the world may hear and receive the good news of the gospel.

One does not really understand the Baptist people until he has attended one other kind of meeting, the church conference in which the whole congregation considers and acts upon the business concerns. In former times, a less busy people would gather on a Saturday afternoon for conference and fellowship; now such meetings are usually combined with others, most often the Wednesday evening service. Here the church elects its officers and the teachers for the Sunday School, adopts a budget for the coming year, hears reports and acts upon recommendations from committees, chooses its messengers to associational or convention meetings, and projects its plans for building. The proceedings are democratic, each member being free to speak his mind, and each being allowed a vote in the decisions. Though the pressures and problems attendant upon all democratic procedures are felt here, we Baptists believe that such procedures are the surest safeguard of our heritage and the best way to preserve the nature of the church, the company in which all believers are priests. No guarantees of justice and truth are built into a democracy, and there is no assurance that the will of the majority will always be the right one, but we act upon the confidence that the company of Christians may best achieve our vocation when we share our insights, and that the humblest member has the right—nay, the obligation, to contribute his judgment and voice to the decisions of the church.

THE RESPONSIBILITIES OF THE CHURCH

The church is a worshipping community. High on the list of our duties as a local church is the obligation to engage in worship. In recognizing this solemn obligation, our primary responsibility is not to a tradition or to historic usages, but to the will of the living Head of the Church. We believe that it is within the competence of the local company of worshippers to determine that will as to times, seasons, and manners of of worship. The variations among Baptist churches in their forms of worship are not a witness to a wilful carelessness but rather a sign of our seeking for the vital and ever-renewed leadership of the Spirit of God.

Similarly, we confess our responsibility to share the good news of new life in Jesus Christ, and within the place where God has set us to serve and to witness we are obliged to give that witness. Even though we work side-by-side with other Christians in the never-ending task of evangelism, and while we rejoice in their effectiveness in their labors, we cannot resign our part of the labor or shift the responsibility to an external ecclesiastical authority.

Further, we believe that the local congregation is competent to choose its own ministers and officers, and otherwise to conduct its own internal affairs. Though decisions may be left to the informed judgment of the pastor or the deacons or a committee, it is the whole congregation that determines what matters are to be left to these, and the congregation chooses the responsible persons.

It is also the duty of the local church to offer instruction and training for its members in the Christian life. Denominational agencies may be able to furnish literature, offer counsel, suggest curricula, and devise effective methods of teaching, but these are servants, not masters, of the Baptist churches. Most of our churches recognize a wide range of areas in which individual Christians need guidance, and one of the most dependable tests of a church's relevance is its readiness to assist its members in vocational decisions, personal spiritual growth, moral choices, and understanding of Christian responsibility in today's world.

A corollary to this is the responsibility of the local church to exercise discipline within its membership. Every congregation includes some who fail, in one way or another, to live up to the high calling of God and who neglect their obligations which they assumed in becoming members. Records of some of the churches of a century ago indicate that most of the business sessions were taken up with the reception of new members and action on the cases of erring ones. The Sandy Creek church in North Carolina, for example, suspended two women from privileges of membership "for being prejidist with each other." A brother was suspended "for refuseing to clare himself of a scandal laid to his charge." Others were suspended or excluded "for the sin of drunkness . . . for an ungodly life in neglect of duty . . . for telling of lyes and calling of God to witness the same . . . for atemting to preach without leave . . . for onjust dealing . . . for being jeoulous of her husband . . . for refuseing to give satisfaction to the church for omition of deuty . . . for refusing sundry times to com to meeting when sighted [cited] to com . . . for clameing a borrow'd bung-borrer as there own."

We have retreated from such strict supervision of the lives of our Church members, and at the same time have almost completely lost the sense of responsibility for discipline. Yet, it is a part of the Baptist insistence upon the local congregation to say that such responsibility does still rest upon the congregation, and that it cannot be shifted, as an unpleasant task, to a nonresident bishop or other distant authority. The Church has the duty and, under God, the authority to maintain a positive and constructive discipline, so that the lives of her members shall truly and faithfully declare the transforming and renewing power of the gospel of Christ.

We deem it to be a part of the local church's obligation to speak of the moral issues in its community, and by her teaching, preaching and acting to provide moral leadership in daily affairs as well as in times of crisis. Larger groups than the

local church, or groups representing Baptists from a wider constituency, such as associations or conventions, may pass resolutions or approve reports dealing specifically with the issues of
the times. Yet, these do not speak for the churches, nor are
their decisions binding upon the churches. We Baptists cannot comfortably point to the decision, for example, of the
Southern Baptist Convention on a resolution calling for the
application of Christian principles in race relations, and be
done with it. We know, and the world knows, that such a
convention action means nothing unless and until it is imple-
mented by the free and responsible action of the churches and
individuals in concrete situations. Here again, then, our claim
to liberty brings with it a responsibility.

Finally, the local church has the liberty, and the responsibility, of deciding how and to what extent it shall participate
in the life of the whole Church, which is the body of Christ.
There is no law among Baptists that requires a congregation
to establish ties with others, or to recognize the work of God
among those who bear another name than our own. Yet an
"independent" Baptist church is an anomaly, because it is a
denial of our heritage, because it is a confession of blindness
to the cause of Christ which is larger than our provincial sympathies and concerns, and because it is a declaration of pride
unbecoming in a people who claim to follow Christ. Since the
congregation is locally governed, however, upon it rests the
responsibility to avoid such pride, blindness, and denial, and
to enter into the fellowship and mission of God's people
throughout the earth, whether they bear the Baptist name or
another.

9

The LARGER FELLOWSHIP

It is not possible to tell the full story of the Baptist people without giving some account of their common life and work beyond the boundaries of the local congregation. The heavy emphasis commonly placed upon the self-government of each community of believers has often obscured this other equally important and complementary aspect of their life and witness. It is true that the local independence has been exaggerated in practice, and there are congregations bearing the Baptist name that make a point of going their own way, disdaining any ties of fellowship or cooperative endeavor with others. But the occasional appearances of such ideas and practices does not negate the stronger and healthier tradition that dates back to the early days of English Baptist history, a tradition that stresses the interdependence of Christians and the fellowship in Christ that scorns the limits of time and space.

Surely no one will claim that we fully exemplify the ideal

of cooperation and fellowship which we profess. Indeed, at times we have so heavily accented our liberty from external control that we have failed to acknowledge, even in our professions, our mutual need and concern. Still it may be asserted that the Baptist genius has found its noblest expression when it has been embodied in cooperation. The Baptists' understanding of the competency of the individual and its correlate, the priesthood of all believers, is saved from an atomizing individualism by this recognition of our need for and our responsibility to each other.

It must be admitted that the New Testament does not offer the detailed guidance in structuring the association which some would desire. While claiming to find in its pages a clear outline of a single and specific polity for the local congregation, some are distressed at being unable to discover the same exact authoritative precedent for associations, societies, and conventions. If the only permissible forms of Christian work are those explicitly set forth in the New Testament, then not only conventions and the like but also many other things now accepted as a normal part of a church's life must be sacrificed. But if we are restricted only to the extent that we must not accept forms which would alter the gospel essentially, having, as we believe, liberty in all others, then the way is open for the adoption of organizational forms as the need of the times may suggest. Fidelity to the New Testament message, not exact duplication of its circumstances and provisions, is the requirement.

Even without the explicit direction of the New Testament in such matters, Baptists have generally recognized the rightness of the inclination toward association with others "of like faith and order." At times this inclination has been strengthened by persecution. Those who suffer unjust legal disabilities are likely to feel a kinship with their fellow-sufferers in the same cause.

More powerful than this motive, however, have been

those impulses toward cooperation which grew out of the positive nature of Baptist life and the task of the church in the world. The earliest Baptist associations in England appear to have arisen out of a conscious sense of need for the edification and inspiration to be gained in such a company. This is a logical extension of the voluntary aspect of church membership. While recognizing that the church is first of all not a voluntary human association, but an aspect of the redemptive work of God, who "setteth the solitary in families," Baptists have seen a special significance in still another aspect, from the human side, of the church's formation. Within the context of God's gracious call and initiative we have, humanly speaking, voluntarily banded ourselves together in responsible obedience to His call and in the interest of His redemptive purpose for all mankind.

THE LARGER BAPTIST FELLOWSHIP

There are three basic approaches to the establishment of intercongregational relations among Baptists. The oldest and most simple of these is the associational approach. In Baptist terminology, an association is an organization formed by several churches for purposes of fellowship and mutual edification and for consideration of matters of common concern. They are usually located fairly close to each other, as, for example, within a single county or in a metropolitan center.

The second approach is that of the society. This is an organization formed by interested persons and groups for the advancement of a particular cause or set of causes. It is not strictly an ecclesiastical body, since individuals, clubs or other groups may have representation in it. Yet, the society has provided the means for Baptist churches to come together in a joint endeavor which is beyond the means of a single congregation to support—a missionary cause, an educational institution, a charitable enterprise, or an effort toward social betterment.

The third approach is that of the convention. This is a more truly denominational organization, in which the churches of like faith and order join both to express their unity in fellowship and to engage in cooperative labors. It thus partakes of some of the qualities of the association and of the society as well. While the name "convention" is applied to this kind of organization by most Baptists in America, and indeed by most Baptists in the whole world, others designate similar organizations as "conferences," "unions," or even "associations." In some respects this is the most important kind of connection for Baptists, since it has become a custom to designate our churches as this or that kind of Baptist churches in terms of the convention or union with which they are affiliated.

The first-mentioned of these patterns of affiliation, the association, is the oldest. It first appears among English Baptists in the days of the Civil Wars:

> The pattern . . . was provided by a military expedient with which Baptists had become familiar during the Civil Wars (1642-49) between King and Parliament. During that first winter, counties were organized into "associations" for defense purposes. . . . In 1653, that part of the Army which was disbanded in Ireland, and which was largely composed of Baptists, transferred this plan to church organization as they sought to maintain fellowship between their lonely congregations in a strange country by correspondence and the frequent meeting of delegates.[1]

The Philadelphia Association, first to be formed in this country, was organized in 1707. During the century others were established all along the eastern seaboard of America. While none of the others became as extensive as the Philadel-

[1] Robert G. Torbet, A *History of the Baptists* (Philadelphia: The Judson Press, 1950), pp. 72 f.

phia Association, and even it did not attempt to be a comprehensive organization for the whole of Baptist life in America, several of these early associations went beyond the purposes of fellowship and inspiration. They raised money for causes that were common to the churches, and some of them sent missionaries on preaching tours in the destitute areas along the western frontier.

The annual or semiannual meeting of the association was formerly the high point in the year for many of our people. They gathered for three or four days as guests of a host church, heard sermons, visited, debated queries that were directed to them, and offered counsel to churches of their number that sought assistance in internal problems. It was a long-continuing custom, both in England and in America, for the association to communicate with all the churches in its fellowship by means of a circular letter which was drawn up by an elected member, then read and approved by the whole company. These letters usually dealt with a theological topic or with some question of more than local interest in the churches' life. They often sparkled with homely wit and keen insight, and much of the advice offered is timely even today. The Western Association in England, meeting at Horsley, Gloucestershire, in 1778, issued a letter which said, in part:

> Be careful that you do not mistake some favorite notion for evangelical truth, natural passion for the work of the spirit, transient conviction for true repentance, a partial reformation for a thorough conversion, an orthodox creed for a living faith, a party spirit for Christian zeal, and a warm imagination for spiritual joy.

In recent years, a tendency has appeared which may mark the end of the old associational idea. The associations are often becoming conventions in miniature; that is, in some cases they are becoming little conventions themselves, denominational agencies, owning property and institutions, and otherwise conducting an extensive program of work with a sizable budget. Under the necessities of reporting on such enterprises and of considering plans and budgets, the associational meetings have become business sessions, in which the elements of fellowship and inspiration are subordinated or lost altogether. In other cases, the association has become a local unit of the state convention or even of the Southern Baptist Convention, for example, and the time of meeting is given over largely to reports on the work of these denominational organizations. The association thus becomes an administrative arm of the larger body, with support and promotion of the work of the larger body as its chief reason for existence and meeting. Such developments are not all loss, to be sure, but they represent a subtle change in the pattern of associative life among our people, and the losses sustained are not being made good in other ways.

The society-type of organization among Baptists also has its roots in English life. In the eighteenth century the formation of societies in England for various worthy enterprises was at its peak. There were such organizations for prison reform, for the improvement of laboring conditions for children, for the abolition of slavery, for foreign missions, and for the translation of the Scriptures. Baptist individuals and churches participated in the work and support of many of these. Thus, it was not a totally strange idea when some Particular Baptist ministers in Northamptonshire proposed, in 1792, the formation of a Baptist society for the propagation of the gospel among the heathen. Within the next 25 years, numerous societies for missionary work were formed, both in England and in America, and the consciousness of a common heritage was enhanced through the sharing of this work under the Baptist name.

These precedents, along with those offered by the general assemblies of both General and Particular Baptists in England, made the formation of comprehensive Baptist organizations that would be nationwide in scope almost inevitable. British Baptists took up the opportunity in a limited fashion in 1813, when a group of ministers formed The General Union of Baptist Ministers and Churches.

In May 1814 a group of 33 delegates in Philadelphia formed The General Missionary Convention of the Baptist Denomination in the United States of America, for Foreign Missions. Here the name "convention" appears for the first time as a label for an American Baptist organization. Though it was formed for the specific purpose of foreign mission work, and though it resembled the older societies in some ways, it was a significant step toward a denominational body.

> It is not the general convention of the societies and other organizations, but of the denomination. . . . It proposes to solicit every Baptist, cuts all the local and partisan limitations, covers the whole denomination. If it had been called the General Society it would have smacked of the limitations of the local societies meeting in it; but it is the Convention, the convening, the coming together, not of societies or churches or other organizations, but of Baptists.[2]

Out of this beginning have grown several conventions in the United States. In 1845 the southern delegates to the general convention withdrew because its mission board refused to appoint as missionary a man who owned slaves, and after their withdrawal led in the formation of the Southern Baptist Convention. The general convention was reorganized as the American Baptist Missionary Union, and it ultimately evolved into the Northern Baptist Convention, since 1950 called the American Baptist Convention. There are two large Negro conventions, the National Baptist Convention of America and the National Baptist Convention of the U. S. A., Incorporated.

It is right and proper at this point to note the existence

[2] Albert L. Vail, *The Morning Hour of American Baptist Missions* (Philadelphia: The Judson Press, 1907), pp. 394 f.

of several other Baptist groups, lest in speaking about these larger bodies we leave the impression that they represent the whole spectrum of Baptist life and thought, or that these others, because they are smaller in number, are unimportant. Some of these maintain a separate identity because of national origins or because a considerable number of their people do not speak English. Typical of these are the Roumanian Baptist Association of America, the Czechoslovak Baptist Convention in America, the Baptist General Conference of America (Swedish in origin), and the North American Baptist General Conference (German).

Still others are concerned with the preservation of a particular theological emphasis, because of which they cannot conscientiously unite with others who do not share their concern. The Primitive Baptists, defenders of a strict Calvinistic doctrine of predestination, are among these. Though their number seems to be diminishing, they still have churches scattered through several states. The late Congressman Sam Rayburn, Speaker of the House of Representatives, united with one of these churches in his later years, and he liked to refer to the American and Southern conventions as "splinter groups."

At the other end of the theological spectrum from the Primitive Baptists, and much more active and strong, are the General Baptists and the Free-Will Baptists. Both of these groups stress the Arminian distinctive doctrines as opposed to hyper-Calvinism.

The very diversity suggested by these names, and the fact that the general organizations in different countries have evolved their own ways of work, make it impossible to describe how Baptists work together in terms that are applicable and accurate in every case. The authors may, however, be forgiven for a kind of provincialism if they choose for a brief description the work of the group which they know best, the Southern Baptist Convention. The choice of this example does not imply that it is a norm for Baptists, or that the ways of the

Baptist Federation of Canada or of the Nigerian Baptist Convention are any less proper or "Baptistic."

The Southern Baptist Convention is composed of individual members who are messengers elected by the churches. Every "regular Baptist church which is in friendly cooperation" with the convention is entitled to elect at least one messenger, and up to ten may be sent, depending upon the size of the church and the amount of its contribution to the work of the convention in the preceding fiscal year. These messengers are not instructed by their churches as to how they shall vote on specific issues before the convention, nor are the actions of the convention binding upon the churches. Article IV of the convention's constitution states: "While independent and sovereign in its own sphere, the Convention does not claim and will never attempt to exercise any authority over any other Baptist body, whether church, auxiliary organization, association, or convention."

The work of the convention is continued in the intervals between annual sessions by its Executive Committee, which operates under specific limitations so that it cannot commit the convention to a course of action that has not been approved by the vote of the whole convention.

The general boards through which Southern Baptists direct their various enterprises are the Foreign Mission Board, Richmond, Virginia; the Home Mission Board, Atlanta, Georgia; the Sunday School Board, Nashville, Tennessee, and the Annuity Board, Dallas, Texas. The convention owns and operates six theological seminaries. There are standing commissions charged with specific concerns, such as the Education Commission, the Historical Commission, the Christian Life Commission, and the Stewardship Commission.

To fulfil its purpose of "eliciting, combining, and directing" the energies of the whole denomination in these tasks, the convention is supported by voluntary gifts made through a financial plan called The Cooperative Program. Each year the Executive Committee hears requests from the various agencies and prepares a tentative budget for the convention, based upon a compromise between the requests of the agencies and the amount that may reasonably be expected in gifts. This budget is presented to the convention's annual session in May or June and adopted, perhaps with modifications.

The task of raising the money to finance these operations then rests upon the individual members in the local churches. No Baptist is assessed any amount, either as membership dues or as his part of the contribution to the denomination's work. Within the local church a budget is usually formed, indicating the amount the church needs for its local expenses and the amount it proposes to give to the Cooperative Program and to other causes. While either the individual or the church may send gifts directly to the convention offices to be divided according to the formula of the year's budget, or to be designated specifically for a certain agency or special cause, most of the money raised is channeled through the work of the state convention, which has its own cooperative program of finance. The state convention follows the same procedure in setting up a budget for the enterprises within the state, such as mission work, schools, hospitals, children's homes, and homes for the aging, and for contributions to the work of the Southern Baptist Convention. Here again the decision is left to the constituency of the convention; the Southern convention does not assess any state convention a certain amount.

While such a voluntary program is beset with some uncertainties, it maintains the freedom of the individual and of the church to interpret the will of God with regard to its stewardship, and it has worked remarkably well. Mr. B, the "typical" Southern Baptist, decides upon the amount he will be able to contribute to his church's work and makes a pledge for that amount. Then, when the church meets in conference to adopt its budget, he joins in the discussion and casts his vote for the division of funds between local causes and those beyond the local community. Part of the latter portion will be given for the work of the association, or designated to some special causes, but probably most of it will go to the Cooperative Program of the state convention. A little later, Mr. B is sent by his church as a messenger to the state convention meeting, and there he shares in the decisions as to how the gifts received from various individuals and churches to the convention will be divided. Much of this money will be used for state work, in support of institutions and agencies within the state, but a large part will be sent, by decision of the state convention, to the Cooperative Program of the Southern Baptist Convention. Mr. B is also a messenger to that convention's annual session, and so again he has a voice in allocating the gifts to different agencies. And the same Mr. B may be elected by one of the conventions as a member of the board of trustees for one of the agencies, and thus may have a voice in the final disposition of the funds which he gave back in his own church. Even though this system of finance depends entirely upon voluntary giving, in 1960 Southern Baptists gave more than $480,000,000 through their churches. Of this amount, over $31,000,000 went for state cooperative program projects, and over $17,000,000 for the Southern Baptist Convention work. Special offerings for home and foreign missions swelled the total given for the Southern Baptist Convention causes to more than $27,000,000 that year.

It should be remembered that, even though the tendency in recent years has been to identify the local church as a certain kind of Baptist church in terms of the convention or other general agency with which it is affiliated, this kind of identification is not strictly accurate. A church may participate in the work of more than one convention, by making contributions and by sending messengers to the sessions. Though this dual alignment is not very widespread, there are churches affiliated with both the Southern Baptist Convention and the American Baptist Convention, or with one of these and at the same time with one of the foreign language bodies. In 1961 the American Baptist Convention reported a total of 695 churches dually aligned.

The most recent development of organizational fellowship among Baptists is the Baptist World Alliance, which met for the first time in 1905. Credit for giving impetus to the idea, and pursuing it until it was taken up by other leaders in England and America, is usually ascribed to J. N. Prestridge, of Louisville, Kentucky. He was not, however, the first to dream of such an assembly. In 1790, John Rippon, of England, had dedicated the first volume of *The Baptist Annual Register* to his brethren in several lands,

> . . . with a desire of promoting an universal interchange of kind offices among them and in serious expectation that before many years elapse (in imitation of other wise men) a deputation from all these climes will meet probably in London to consult the ecclesiastical good of the whole. . . .

Others had advanced the proposal from time to time in the nineteenth century, but it was not until 1904, under the influence of the most prominent Baptists on both sides of the Atlantic, that the decision was made to call a meeting for the following year.

Plans were made for meetings at 5-year intervals, and although wars and other emergencies have forced postponement more than once, the Alliance has continued to meet and to grow. In the tenth meeting, held in Rio de Janeiro in 1960, more than 12,000 delegates from 72 countries attended.

Through the offices of the Alliance, Baptists of various countries are able to keep in touch with one another and to share strength and leadership. It is difficult for those of us in the United States, where we enjoy freedom of worship and where we are so numerous, to conceive of the difficulties in which our brethren of other lands live and work. Nevertheless, we are able to share in their joys, welcome their achievements, and sense a tie with them even though we have not seen them. The Baptist fellowship is still growing. Reports have come recently of eighteen Vietnamese converts who were baptized in March 1962, the first Baptists in that country. In the Rio meeting, in a single session, the delegates and visitors heard testimonies from fellow-Baptists from the U.S.S.R., Pakistan, Liberia, and Cuba. Our denominational papers carry reports of new churches in Nigeria, of the addition of three hundred members to Dutch Baptist churches, of the publication of a new hymnal by our brethren in Hungary, and of the formation of a Baptist convention in Lebanon. Through such acquaintance, through prayer for one another, and through our sharing in the life of the body of Christ, we are able to bear our Christian witness and, in the words of the letter of the Welsh Association in 1790, "as well to brighten the golden chain of Fellowship."

THE LARGER FELLOWSHIP OF ALL CHRISTIANS

The same John Rippon mentioned above said, in the preface to his first volume of the *Register:*

> Though I feel it an honour to rank with the Calvinists, whose system, commonly called orthodox, is peculiarly dear to me; yet conceiving that all who hate sin, and love our Lord Jesus Christ in sincerity, are good men, if they do not think of Baptism as I do, nor embrace half my Creed, I delight in such as my brethren, and embrace them, by thousands, in the bosom of warm affection—and, with my views, it would be criminal not to do so. . . .

Such a sympathetic concern for other Christians has not been universal among Baptists. Seventeenth century Baptist literature abounds with the sharpest criticisms of "papists," "paedobaptists," and others. Yet it must be remembered that the Baptists had suffered, and were still suffering, often severe persecution at the hands of these Christian brothers. It would have been a rare fulfilment of the gospel injunction if they had returned good for that kind of evil.

Yet, before that century expired, much of that bitterness had vanished, and the spirit of John Rippon could possess a large number of our people. It is likely that this mellowing came earlier in the centers of population than on the frontier. In 1767, Francis Alison, Presbyterian minister in Philadelphia, could write: "I am well acquainted with many of the Baptists, . . . and can testify that they are sober, religious, candid and friendly to all other denominations, and deserve all Christian regard, as worthy members of Christ's universal church." This mutual esteem appeared, too, on the mission field, and William Carey tells of having authorized a paedobaptist missionary to draw on the Baptist missionaries' account if he should find himself in need.

In the twentieth century, the great opportunity for interdenominational cooperation has come in the ecumenical movement. Baptists from various countries participated in the International Missionary Council, the Conferences on Life and Work, and those on Faith and Order. Some Baptist groups belong to the National Council of Churches, and still more, of course, to the World Council of Churches.

Yet, some of our people have remained aloof from the main stream of contemporary Christian life, at least as far as its organizational forms are concerned. The Southern Baptist Convention's repeated rejection of any affiliation with these national and world councils has occasioned much comment and criticism. We are called, largely because of this refusal, the "problem child of American Protestantism." Even as we move into the latter half of the twentieth century, this spirit of isolation from other Christian bodies seems to be increasing. It may be attributed in part to our general cultural isolation, a far more powerful reality in our lives than we commonly recognize. It is partially due, too, to our congregational polity, which serves both as reason and excuse for our failing to join the ecumenical movement. Still another reason is the increasing insistence, in some quarters, upon doctrinal agreement as the basis for Christian fellowship. The fears that our Baptist witness would be compromised by our joining these councils, while unconfirmed, are nonetheless real.

It has often been noted that this spirit of isolationism is particularly strong where Baptists have been influenced by the "Landmark movement" which appeared in the mid-nineteenth century in the South. J. R. Graves, the father of the movement, was a pastor, editor, and controversialist whose writing and speaking helped to mold the ecclesiology of Baptists in the middle South and the Southwest. Graves refused to recognize the churches other than Baptist as true churches, calling them only "religious societies." It followed from this that their ministers were not properly ordained, and that their acts as ministers were not valid. The validity of Baptist claims, on the other hand, could be demonstrated, according to the Landmarkers' view, by two things: the adherence of present-day Baptist churches to the New Testament faith and order, and the exhibition of a line of churches in historical succession (or, more accurately, of properly baptized individuals) from the time of the apostles to the present. Early in this century a division in the Southern Baptist Convention occurred over these Landmark principles and related side issues. A new general body, the American Baptist Association, was formed of those who held these ideas and insisted upon them as a basis for fellowship. This group divided again in 1950, and the North American Baptist Association was formed as a result. Both of these groups advocate the ideas of Graves and his followers. Yet, this departure has not removed from the Southern Baptist Convention the force of the Landmark movement. Graves' ecclesiology is still present, and probably even dominant, in the Southwest and the Far West.

In spite of these tendencies to isolate us, there is still co-operation between Southern Baptists and others on the local level. As in other cases, convention action, or failure to act, in this matter is not binding upon the local churches. Individuals and churches do participate in city and state councils of churches as opportunities appear. Combined services with other churches are held, and Baptist pastors belong to ministerial associations with their fellow-laborers of other denominations.

To the appeals for reunion of the churches Baptists respond in a more nearly uniform way. While acknowledging the desirability of reunion, we are convinced that it is not to be gained by the sacrifice of Biblical truth, nor by concessions made by the free churches to those which depend upon an episcopal succession alone. The Assembly of the British Baptist Union in 1926 responded to the Lambeth Appeal of the Anglican Church in a notable and eloquent defense of the Baptist position:

> We believe in the Catholic Church as the holy Society of believers in our Lord Jesus Christ, which He founded, of which He is the only Head, and in which He dwells by His Spirit, so that though made up of many communions, organized in various modes, and scattered throughout the world, it is yet one in Him. . . .

> It will be gathered from this reply that union of such a kind as the Bishops have contemplated is not possible for us. . . . Further progress in the direction of Christian unity can be secured, we are convinced, only by unreserved mutual recognition. . . . We believe that the time has come when the Churches of Christ should unite their forces to meet the need of the world. We therefore are prepared to join the Church of England in exploring the possibility of a federation

of equal and autonomous Churches in which the several parts of the Church of Christ would co-operate in bringing before men the will and claims of our Lord.[3]

It was this firm conviction that led the Executive Committee of the Baptist World Alliance to decide not to encourage an invitation to send observers to the Second Vatican Council of the Roman Catholic Church, assembled in Rome in October 1962. Discussions and decisions of the council will undoubtedly have great significance for future steps toward union among the churches, and even though we did not send observers, Baptists have followed the proceedings with interest and with prayers for divine leadership of all who participate.

Nowhere is the inability for one Baptist to speak for all Baptists more obvious than in this area. Our attitudes toward the life and work of fellow-Christians range all the way from utter indifference, or even unseemly competition, to passionate involvement and eager desire for unity and union. For most of our people, both in theory and in practice, the Baptist position is somewhere between these two extremes. Without attempting to foretell the course of future events, it may be fair for us as individual Baptists to express the hope that, as we come more clearly to see that all Christians worship and serve the same Lord, we may also see more clearly that we belong to each other.

[3] *Quoted by* A. C. Underwood, *A History of English Baptists* (London: Kingsgate Press, 1947), pp. 261 ff.

EVANGELISM and EDUCATION

Since Baptists stress personal religious experience as essential for Christian discipleship, and as prerequisite for church membership, evangelism is sometimes called the life-blood of our churches. The figure of speech is a well-chosen one. Coursing through the whole body of the church, it serves both to nourish and to purge. Where a defective or unwholesome evangelism is practiced, the result is spiritual anemia in the churches, or a disease which is quickly carried to every part of the body. On the other hand, a healthy evangelism imparts vigor to every other aspect of the life of the churches.

A strong and defensible program of evangelism, of course, does not aim at a single initial decision and no more. It rather strives for a continuing renewal of personal commitment to God in Christ, a development of God-given talents and opportunities for his service, an interpretation of every relationship and responsibility of life in the light of the Christian faith, and a lifelong growth in Christian maturity. The full and final intention of evangelism requires, for its achievement, the work of teaching and training.

It is appropriate, then, that we consider in a single chapter these two ways in which Baptists do their work, for although they may be distinguishable in some respects, evangelism and education are closely connected and mutually dependent. They are twin supports, and twin responsibilities, of our churches.

THE EVANGELISTIC ENTERPRISE

In spite of our intense interest in the matter, and in spite of our heavy emphasis upon it, Baptists cannot claim to have invented evangelism, nor do we have a monopoly on it today. The early Christian witnesses described their message about Jesus Christ as the *euangelion*, "good news." The written witnesses to the meaning of Jesus and his ministry also bore the same name; they are the Gospel, the *euangelion*, according to Matthew, Mark, Luke, John. In our own day we use a derivative of this word to name this, our central task: to share with others the good news which is God's call to man in Christ, a call which is both gift and challenge, both warning and promise. This task belongs to all Christians, not to Baptists alone, and not alone to those who perform a special ministry of evangelistic preaching.

We share with other Christians, too, the methods by which this work is done. One immediately thinks of the revival meeting, or preaching mission, which in some circles is still equated with the whole evangelistic labor of the church. Along with others, however, we practice visitation evangelism, in which a pastor, or some other worker, will seek out the unenlisted at home or at work and, in personal conversation, lay before them the claims of Christ upon their lives and the invitation of the gospel. Facilities of radio and television, and of the printed word in various forms, are also used to gain entrance to remote and hard-to-reach places and thus to extend the invitation. Among Southern Baptist churches, at least, the Sunday School is an evangelistic agency. Some of our churches report that as many as 80 percent of their new members come to their decisions to unite with the church through the ministry of the Sunday School.

In frontier days, our Baptist churches enjoyed the benefits and suffered the problems offered by the camp-meeting. For many communities, where no settled ministry was available, these meetings offered the only opportunity to hear the gospel preached. A twentieth century audience, surfeited with preaching, may consider this no great attraction. Yet the contemporary accounts of these meetings almost consistently speak of the opportunity as a precious one. Other elements of appeal, of course, were not lacking. The camp-meeting was a great social occasion for the community in which it was held, and for others for miles around.

As the camp-meetings became less common, the local churches continued the practice of having extended periods of special evangelistic services, "protracted meetings," or revivals. This practice is almost universal among Baptist churches in America down to the present time, though the local usages vary considerably.

The ministry of the travelling evangelist is not a thing of the past, though its critics have heavily scored it, and though abuses of its opportunities have been all too numerous. The work of Billy Graham, the best-known of such evangelists today, has done much to restore the good name of mass evangelism. Though Graham is a Baptist, his crusades are usually under the sponsorship of churches of several denominations. Members of his team are insistent upon the church relationship as a vital factor in genuine evangelism, and those who make decisions during the crusades are encouraged to follow through with membership in a church where they can worship and work.

In many Baptist churches, every service is an evangelistic effort, and at the close of the service an invitation is issued for hearers to make a public profession of their faith. Here the songs, Scripture readings, and sermons are consciously chosen with this end in view. The evangelistic sermon usually treats of man's sin and guilt, God's mercy and forgiveness, His claim upon our lives, the challenge of the Christian life, and the need for personal commitment in repentance and faith.

Preaching for decision is crucially important in the evangelistic effort. It reflects the importance which Baptists attribute to preaching in general. At the same time, it underscores our belief in the priesthood of all believers. In this context, this belief takes the form of an insistence that no authority external to the person can decide on his behalf for or against his Christian commitment—neither minister, nor parent, nor official of the state, nor law, nor custom. Evangelistic preaching is aimed at the very citadel of the soul, seeking that personal decision which no one else can make, and which, when made, no other person can abrogate.

Baptists have a "relish for savoury experimental preaching," as it was said of a noble eighteenth century Baptist woman. Such preaching dwells upon the inward and external effects of conversion. It elicits confidence in the unfailing goodness of God and encourages believers to share with each other their joys and their doubts.

Attention is often called to the dangers of emotionalism engendered in an evangelistic service, in which a shallow and fleeting emotion may be mistaken for a genuine conversion of one's whole perspective and manner of life. This is particularly perilous when appeals are made to young children, or when they are accompanied by the "gimmicks" of crowd psychology. Overzealous ministers and teachers have sometimes exacted professions of faith from children too young and immature to understand the nature of the choice urged upon them. To use cajolery, or to resort to fear, the desire to please the teacher, or the wish to go along with the crowd as motive forces in such a context, is unworthy to be called evangelism, and it may lead to irreparable harm. Older people, too, may be tricked into a profession which they do not intend.

Yet, the good name of evangelism survives among Baptists. Indeed, never in our history has it enjoyed such wide attention and such intensive study as we are devoting to it today. Various state and national conventions are initiating programs of evangelism that are soundly Biblical. Sensitive to the criticisms, and aware of the dangers of a frivolous and statistically-oriented "soul-winning," leaders in these offices are showing the way to re-invest evangelism with its rightful primacy among the tasks of the Christian church.

In seminary classrooms, too, young ministers are studying evangelism in new dimensions of breadth and depth. There have been instances when the seminary course in evangelism was nothing more than the memorization of the proper verses of the Bible to quote in meeting doubts or objections of nonbelievers. We have come to see, however, that this is no longer effective, if it ever was, and that it encourages a superficiality of profession which is the antithesis of true evangelism. Today's evangelist must possess much more than a store of memorized verses; he must have an understanding of the psychology of religious experience and conversion, an insight into the ethical implications of the gospel, and an ability to sympathize with, and to respect, the doubts of the person with whom he works. The use of these resources by a Christian witness whose own life bears evidence of transformation and who is prompted by compassion and zeal to give his testimony can mean a new resurgence of healthy evangelism.

THE EDUCATIONAL ENTERPRISE

Baptists are interested in education. To be convinced of this, one only need look at the long list of schools, academies, colleges, and seminaries which our people have founded and support around the world; or at the literature which pours from the presses of various Baptist bodies, or at the intensive educational activity of multitudes of local churches. In fact, some of our state conventions allot a larger amount of their budget for educational institutions than for any other single aspect of their work.

The local congregations' educational effort may be seen in the Sunday School and other such activities, in programs of weekday education in some of our churches, in the teaching ministry of the pastor, and in the increasing frequency and importance of a full-time ministry of Christian education.

We have already mentioned the role of the Sunday School as an agency of evangelism. It must be understood, however, that its purpose goes far beyond that of finding and enlisting people in Christian discipleship and church membership. It is, in fact, the educational agency of the local church. Better still, it *is* the church at study, the church learning as well as teaching. Some Baptist churches—for example, most of those in Great Britain—have provision in the Sunday School only for the children and young people. In America, however, it is common for the Sunday School to be arranged with classes for all age groups. Nurseries are provided for infants. For other small children, there are departments where the love of God is taught, not in conceptual forms but in experiences of playing, singing, storytelling, and sharing. At the age where such study is feasible, the study of Biblical material is introduced, and this becomes the basic text material for classes on up through the adult level. The teaching is done, except in rare instance, by unpaid workers who are elected by the church. The tremendous opportunities and responsibilities inherent in this work are illustrated by the fact that, in 1960, Southern Baptist churches had more than 7,200,000 people enrolled in their Sunday Schools.

Without discounting the importance of other educational activities, it may be suggested that the Sunday School, because of its ministry to the whole age span, its appeal to church members and nonmembers alike, and its close tie to the continuing life of the whole church, is the most important single aspect of our educational work. John Mason Peck, Baptist missionary to the frontier country, established Sunday schools as he moved westward, and, in a report in 1824 to the sponsoring agency, told of his own views as to their significance: "That these institutions will become nurseries of piety, virtue, and intelligence in Missouri and Illinois, and that the effect will be visible ages hence, I have no doubt."

The local churches do engage in other forms of educational work, however, specifically related to their own work, the meaning of the Christian life, the world-wide mission of the church, and various contemporary issues. The programs for such training of church members vary greatly from one Baptist group to another, and most groups use more than a single method. A church may, for example, have all of the following programs of teaching, in addition to the Sunday School, running concurrently: a training program for the church membership, adapted to various age groups and continued throughout the year, meeting, for example, before the Sunday evening service; a program of missionary education, designed to stimulate support for the denomination's mission work and to acquaint the church members with various mission fields, missionary problems, and personnel; a week's concentrated program of training for workers in some particular aspect of church work, Bible study, Christian history, educational methods, or ethical responsibility. This diversified program of teaching is not unusual, but quite common, even in smaller churches. Its development is part of the reason for the increasing demand for ministers of Christian education in our churches. The demand itself is reflected in the growth of schools for training these ministers, either in connection with theological seminaries or as separate institutions.

The most important single motivation in our founding of various schools and colleges, in fact, has been the desire to train ministers for our churches. While Baptists and other dissenters were barred from study in the English universities, no other course than the establishment of their own schools appeared possible for such training to be provided. Even when these barriers were removed, and in America where they were not thus rigidly applied, this motive still sufficed for Baptists to begin their own institutions for the schooling of ministers. The Triennial Convention, in 1820, addressed itself to this challenge:

> Though the first object which engaged our attention was the great and blessed work of sending the gospel to the heathen, it soon occurred that, in connexion with this, God had other important services for us to fulfil.
>
> Surely if there be any suitable means, that can be employed in a manner consistent with the will of God, for obtaining a more ample supply of useful ministers; to employ these means with care and diligence, must appear of high importance. . . .
>
> It is the belief of this Convention, that there are such means; means, not only lawful, but furnished by Divine Providence for the very purpose. . . .
>
> Ministers, according to our sentiments, must be gracious men, renewed and sanctified by the Spirit of God; they must possess gifts from Christ for their office; and must be called of God to engage in it. But these gifts they may either neglect or improve. . . .

Even before this time, Baptists had encouraged the training of their ministers in existing schools. Thomas Hollis, II, a Baptist merchant of London, had given a sum to underwrite the expenses of two young men who were to train for the ministry in Harvard. The Philadelphia Association had sought to raise money for support of an academy at Hopewell, New Jersey, and after that school closed, directed its energies toward the development of a general educational fund. The Association was influential, too, in securing a charter for Rhode Island College, now Brown University, which began under Baptist auspices.

By the year 1825, educational societies had been formed in several states for the support of institutions and of individual students. Baptists had founded The Maine Literary and Theological Institution, later to become Colby College; Newton Theological Institution, later to be merged into the present-day Andover-Newton; Columbian College, in the nation's capital, and other less well-known schools.

Although some of these schools were founded for the express purpose of training ministers, and this purpose was included in the plans for others, most of them were quite broad in scope. This tradition has been continued in Baptist colleges and universities down to the present. They not only have the various academic departments for undergraduate study in arts and sciences, but several of them also maintain professional schools in law, medicine, and nursing. In 1962, Southern Baptists were operating 32 senior colleges and 19 junior colleges, as well as 7 academies. In addition, 7 new colleges were in various stages of planning. These are generally owned and operated by the several state conventions. In the American Baptist Convention, there were 24 senior colleges, 5 junior colleges, and 6 academies, though some of these sustained an undefined relationship with the denomination.

These schools have usually embodied a two-fold method of achieving their mission: 1) they intend to offer training, in the whole range of the academic curriculum, in a "Christian atmosphere"—that is, in a context of Christian commitment, where Christian faith is not only permitted but encouraged, and where values cherished by the Christian church are honored, and 2) they teach (and often require) courses in Bible, or in some other subject specifically related to religious concerns.

We are not ashamed of our heavy emphasis upon the Bible. We believe in its relevance, not only for the ordering of the life and work of the Church, but also for guidance in individual lives and relationships. It should not be surprising that we make it a part of the "core curriculum" in our schools, as well as in the teaching agencies of the local churches.

This same central emphasis upon the Bible is seen, not only in the colleges, but more particularly in our theological institutions. Among American Baptists, these schools are sometimes affiliated with universities as one of the graduate schools, but more often they are constituted as independent institutions, theological seminaries, under separate administration. In either kind, of course, the curriculum includes much in other fields in addition to study of the Bible. A typical program of study in one of these seminaries might include the Biblical languages, both broad and intensive study of the Old and New Testaments, Biblical archaeology, the history of Christianity, systematic theology, Christian ethics and sociology, missionary history and practice, the educational work of the Church, worship, preaching, comparative study of religions, and the history and special teachings of various Christian denominations, including our own.

The normal course of study presupposes a college or university degree. It is expected that this course will have prepared the student for theological study, through courses in language and literature, history, philosophy, and the sciences. Both classical and modern languages are valuable parts of this preparation. Most of our Baptist seminaries in America are fully accredited by the American Association of Theological Schools, and many of them recommend the program of pre-theological study as outlined by the Association. The standard theological course itself is normally three years in length, leading to the Bachelor of Divinity degree. Some of the schools offer additional work beyond this, leading to a master's or a doctor's degree in theology.

Several of our seminaries maintain a program of non-degree study for those who do not have the collegiate preparation for the B. D. program, and there are even separate institutions, sometimes called Bible institutes or training schools, established to minister to the needs of these men. Even though the educational level of Baptist ministers is steadily rising, the demand for courses of study at the non-degree level is likely to continue for some years to come.

Our Baptist brethren in Great Britain also maintain their own schools for training ministers, though in recent years a closer connection with the universities has developed. Regent's Park College is now recognized as one of the colleges of Oxford University. Spurgeon's College in London, founded by the great evangelist-pastor, who did not himself have the advantages of higher education, is a significant part of the life of English churches. Spurgeon was willing to take young men who had insufficient background for a full theological course and train them, even in rudimentary principles, but he did not expect them to stop short of high academic attainments. He insisted that they should study Latin, Greek, and Hebrew, and he sometimes said that a man was not finally fitted for the ministry until he could read the Old and New Testaments in the original languages. Such high standards were not peculiar to him, of course, and British Baptists have been noted generally for their devotion to thorough scholarship in Biblical studies.

It would not be correct, of course, to assume that this concern is uniformly strong, or that we claim that we have resolved all the conflicts between religious faith and intellectual pursuits. Among Baptists, as among other denominations, one may find suspicion of schools and educated men. It is sometimes thought that the schools, even the seminaries, are out of touch with the churches and that the "ivory tower" charge is justified. Our schools do not always conform to the wishes of the people who support them, and the educators are not always articulate in explaining their work and their understanding of the educational endeavor. Most of our schools are not given adequate financial support for the programs which their constituents expect them to fulfil. Even in those instances where the institutions are firmly attached to our denomination, and boards of control are elected by convention or union, friction sometimes develops. Differences over the nature, extent, and importance of academic freedom beset some of our schools. There are disagreements about control of student life and conduct. Some Baptists wish to exercise stricter control over the content and method of teaching, particularly in our theological seminaries, and some believe that nothing ought to be taught in our schools which is not in harmony with the opinions of a majority of our constituency. In spite of our Baptist belief in freedom and the absence of creedal norms of doctrine, heresy trials are still a possibility. In some Baptist circles it still is dangerous to teach the documentary hypothesis as explaining the structure of the Pentateuch, even though it has been taught in virtually all our schools for many years.

Nevertheless, in spite of some reverses, the cause of education among Baptists is prospering, and advances are steadily being made toward a more responsible educational endeavor.

Perhaps these disagreements are growing pains of a people striving for maturity. We cannot long evade the challenge to "learn the way of the Lord more perfectly" and to face with utter honesty every question of the human intellect. We shall not retreat from the task of education: "that the man of God may be mature, fully equipped for every kind of noble work."

MISSIONS
And WORKS of MERCY

The story of the Christian missionary adventure was an old and honorable one when Baptists first appeared on the scene. Beginning with the first generation, Christian witnesses, impelled by ineffable wonder at the gift of God's grace, had gone out to share the good news with others. They had crossed cultural boundaries, surmounted unexpected barriers, endured hardship and resistance, and conquered some of their own inner fears and deep prejudices in the fulfilment of their calling.

Yet at the beginning of the seventeenth century, when the first Baptist churches are found, Protestants were not engaged in missionary activity. The Reformation was not yet a century old, and Europe, the center of Christendom, was still afflicted with the wars of religion. England's church was struggling unsuccessfully with the demands for further reform. Puritan, Independent, Separatist—each added his voice to the clamor. It is not surprising that little energy was left for a more constructive effort in such a context as this.

Neither of the two major groups of early English Baptists was at first concerned with missionary responsibility. Such a concern was not the main thrust of their distinctiveness, and indeed in this respect they did not at all advance beyond the position of their contemporaries. Hence the story of the denomination and the story of our missionary effort do not exactly coincide.

The missionary story itself is an uneven one. It begins with apparent indifference to all missionary opportunities. Then modest efforts were put forth by individuals, churches, and associations. These efforts were directed to domestic missions. In America, for example, they ministered to the spiritual needs of destitute communities, usually those on the advancing frontier. Next came the society plan of supporting mission work, already described. This novel plan evoked serious opposition from some, and in the same context the very missionary enterprise itself was seriously contested. Gradually, however, missionary organizations were perfected and sentiment in favor of a world mission was created. The great majority of Baptists today, in whatever convention, union, or conference they may be joined, engage in mission work of some kind, and the anti-mission group is diminishing in numbers and in influence. This phase of expanding mission work covers the past 160 years of Baptist life in America, and it began in England a decade earlier. Its story includes the accounts of missionaries themselves and the agencies at home supporting them.

The reasons for our initial indifference to missions are not difficult to see. External circumstances alone might have been sufficient to account for it. During most of the first half-century of Baptist life, our people were literally fighting for their very existence. Whatever missionary zeal the people may have had could easily be deployed in convincing and converting those who aggressively opposed them on ecclesiastical and political grounds.

There were theological reasons for the indifference to missions, too, among the Particular Baptists. These people were stout Calvinists. It was fundamental to their theological system that Christ had died only for the sake of the elect (hence his atoning work was "particular" rather than "general"). God's predestinating grace is extended only to those who are chosen by his immutable will. That will is not thwarted, no matter what efforts man may employ or what resistance he may exert to the contrary. Missionary work when addressed to the elect is unnecessary; when directed to the nonelect, unavailing. It is from this perspective that William Carey was answered when he arose to ask, "Is nothing then to be done?" The answer, if brusque, was theologically consistent: "Sit down, young man. When God gets ready to convert the heathen, he will do it without your help or mine."

Still another reason for our failure to develop a strong sense of missionary urgency is the fact that there were mission societies already at work before Baptists in general were awake to their obligations. Through these other channels, our people could manifest and implement their concern, and yet not appreciably affect their own communion, or move it toward its own distinctive missionary endeavor.

By the end of the eighteenth century a definite change had occurred, and Baptists generally were ready to undertake mission work on a rather wide scale. What had happened? In the first place, persecution and legal disabilities of Baptists, both in England and in America, had generally ended. This relief permitted the energies of our people to be turned toward positive efforts of evangelization. A second significant change was the theological modification among Particular Baptists. No leader was more effective in this regard than Andrew Fuller, pastor at Kettering, Northamptonshire, in England, from 1782 to 1815. Though opposed by the hyper-

Calvinists of his own fellowship, he preached, wrote, and argued effectively for a Baptist missionary effort, and much of the early success of the Baptist Missionary Society is due to his labors.

A third change responsible for Baptist missionary work is the development of a denominational consciousness. The associations, though they were not originally formed for missionary work, contributed to this consciousness, and in many cases they began sponsoring missionaries as a natural and proper part of their work.

Even though American Baptists had begun some mission work in the frontier settlements and among the Indians as early as 1760, it was in England that the decisive and dramatic step in Baptist missions was first taken. The story begins with a meeting of the ministers in the Northamptonshire Association in 1791. There William Carey, who earned his living by making shoes and teaching school while serving as pastor of a small Baptist church, asked his fellow-pastors a disturbing question. He invited them to consider "whether it was not practicable, and our bounden duty, to attempt somewhat toward spreading the gospel to the Heathen World." In pursuit of the matter, a few months later he published his booklet, *An Enquiry into the Obligations of Christians to Use Means for the Conversion of the Heathens.* Encouraged by others to preach his convictions on the subject, when the association met on May 31, 1792, he delivered his now-famous sermon, "Expect great things from God; attempt great things for God," using Isaiah 54:2-3 as his text. It was agreed that the next meeting of the ministers, to be held at Kettering in October of the same year, should consider ways of responding to this challenge. There a group of twelve men formed "The Particular Baptist Society for Propagating the Gospel among the Heathen," later to be called the "Baptist Missionary Society."

Carey's work did not end here. He strenuously cultivated

the concern, by preaching and writing, and sought to raise funds for the Society's work. Then, in the following year, when the time came for the first missionaries to be sent out, he offered himself for service in India. Carey quickly became the personal embodiment of missionary work in foreign lands, not only for English Baptists but for those in America as well. For 43 years he stayed and worked, and before the end of his life he had won acceptance as university teacher, linguist, botanist, and advisor to government authorities.

Above all else, Carey is remembered as a missionary statesman. He maintained a voluminous correspondence with English and American friends, and his letters, published and widely distributed, were a major factor in stimulating support for enlarged missionary efforts. His breadth of vision was remarkable. Very early he saw that simply to preach to the Indian people would not be enough to achieve the desired effects of the Christian gospel. He sought, therefore, to employ every possible means to reach larger numbers, through the printed word, by works of mercy, and in educational institutions. His work in translation and in compiling dictionaries was of staggering proportions. He urged the American Baptists to send a medical missionary to join him. In order to make the mission more self-sufficient, he obtained the necessary information and built a paper mill to supply paper for Bibles, textbooks, and newspapers. Typical of his letters was one in which he asked the Society to send out "a serious man who understands the manufacture of glazed earthenware." In his judgment, no honorable labor was alien to the missionary enterprise, if only it would contribute in some way to the cause of sharing the good news of the Christian gospel with others.

In America, too, the fires of missionary zeal were burning more brightly as the eighteenth century came to a close. Carey's work had become known, and a considerable sum in support of his work had been given by American contributors, before American Baptists began to send their own missionaries to the foreign fields of service. In 1802, members of two Boston churches formed the Massachusetts Baptist Missionary Society, for the purpose of supporting circuit-riding preachers in needy parts of this country. The society's magazine regularly printed reports from the English missionaries in India. Other societies began to be formed all along the eastern seaboard, most of them for the purpose of raising funds in support of missionary endeavors. There were several "Female Cent" societies, and "Children's Cent" societies, the members of which pledged themselves to contribute a penny each week, or at other stated intervals, for this cause. There were some who objected to these new organizations, since no warrant for them could be found in the Scriptures. One critic strongly denounced the notion "that the work of Almighty God should be thought to be dependent upon the efforts of American females!" In spite of the critics, however, the interest in the mission societies grew, and it was only a matter of time until Baptists in America should recognize their responsibility to preach the gospel to those in other lands. The issue was to be presented to our people in an unexpected and inescapable fashion.

We have already described those events connected with the development of the General Missionary Convention. This, of course, was only the beginning of American Baptists' active participation in the world mission of the church. For a generation, Adoniram Judson personified this participation, even after many others had been sent to join him and to work in other fields. As it so often goes with pioneers, his work was difficult and dangerous. After five years of labor, he wrote to a minister in London:

> It is painful to write, as usual, that no Burman has yet been brought to the knowledge of the truth. Yet so it is. We now and then discover something hopeful, but it passes away. We are breaking up the ground, and beginning to sow the

precious seed. O may the Lord display his power and change the face of this barren wilderness!

Judson and his wife endured threats and imprisonment again and again. In spite of stout opposition, they followed the counsel of Carey, that "missionaries must knock loud and push hard at the door, and if there be the smallest opening, must force themselves in." Judson lived to see his labors begin to bear fruit, and the presence of a strong community of Baptists in Burma today is a testimony to his faithfulness and courage, and to the work of others in each succeeding generation since that time.

The career of Adoniram Judson ended in 1850, when he died on board ship and was buried at sea. In a letter to his sister, Mrs. Judson tells of his burial and at the same time sums up his career:

> They lowered him into his ocean grave, without a prayer; for his freed spirit had soared above the reach of earthly intercession, and to the foreigners who stood around, it would have been a senseless form. And there they left him in his unquiet sepulchre; but it matters little, for we know that while the unconscious clay is "drifting on the shifting currents of the restless main," nothing can disturb the hallowed rest of the immortal spirit. Neither could he have a more fitting monument, than the blue waves which visit every coast; for his warm sympathies went forth to the ends of the earth, and included the whole family of man.

The story of Judson is of particular meaning to American Baptists, since it is more than a tale of heroism. It is an initial chapter of our continuing and expanding world missionary enterprise, which today touches every continent.

While the pioneer missionaries were pouring out their lives in faraway places, their fellow Baptists here at home were not idle, but were gathering their resources for support and expansion of the work. Luther Rice, companion of the Judsons, shared their experience of coming to a Baptist persuasion, and while they remained on the mission field, he returned home to stir up the American Baptist churches to acceptance and support of their new and unsought opportunity. He travelled almost constantly, visiting churches and associations, and spoke and wrote extensively on behalf of missions. The General Missionary Convention, organized in 1814, was itself a tribute to his zeal. This, however, was only the beginning. Rice continued to plead for more missionaries, wider vision, larger gifts, and a broader base of support for the cause.

Yet, even the convention, which in Rice's view seemed essential, was not universally accepted among Baptists. Little centers of anti-mission, or anti-convention sentiment, appeared, most of them among Baptists on the frontier.

One of the most colorful and powerful opponents of Baptist mission work was Daniel Parker, a preacher who worked in Georgia, Tennessee, Illinois, and Texas. Parker's distinctive views are summarized in the name of the group which he led, who called themselves the Two-Seed-in-the-Spirit Predestinarian Baptists. An effective preacher and able controversialist, he revived a doctrine reminiscent of the ancient Manichaeans', and held that while some men are God's creation, others are begotten of Satan, and these latter are, of course, nonelect. He believed the work of missionary societies and other such human inventions to be contrary to the divine plan, and claimed that churches have no business supporting these schemes, that the indulgence in such un-Biblical practices constitutes a sufficient basis for breaking fellowship.

Mission work received a bad name in some places, too, because of some unscrupulous travellers who claimed to be missionaries, thus gaining access to churches and exploiting their hospitality. *The Massachusetts Baptist Missionary Magazine* says that the account of these missionary impostors "would make a book of no inconsiderable size, but of a sable hue." It then gives a graphic picture of their behavior.

> The following will generally be found as very sure marks by which an impostor may be known. A large bundle of letters, mostly from scattering individuals, but not public characters, and none of them directly to the point. He has lately been sick at a great expense, met with great losses, been badly cheated, has a poor horse, or none at all, and is out of money. He tells marvellous stories of what he has done and suffered, and very confused and improbable ones about the place he is from and that to which he is bound.

These negative influences and the efforts of men like Parker were not enough to suppress the rising sentiment in favor of a strenuous missionary endeavor. The General Missionary Convention prospered, and until the unfortunate division in 1845 over the question of slavery it gave promise of serving as the national organization of Baptists. After this division, both the northern and the southern groups continued to maintain a central missionary emphasis, and today's American Baptist Convention and the Southern Baptist Convention give a major part of their attention and their contributions to missionary causes.

The American Baptist Convention, for example, incorporates the work of general home and foreign mission societies, as well as women's societies. It continues the work of the old General Missionary Convention, though several changes in organization have occurred in the past century and more. Around the center of interest afforded by this missionary concern, a denominational body has grown up, and the convention now incorporates the shared responsibilities of Baptists in a number of areas other than missions.

The Southern Baptist Convention was organized specifically for foreign mission work. Even in the organization, however, provision was made for the inclusion of other kinds of work in which Baptists of the South might cooperate. On the basis of this provision, Southern Baptists have taken up extensive labors in educational institutions, publishing enterprises, charitable causes, and programs of assistance to local congregations, as well as missionary causes at home and abroad.

Baptists actively participate in a world-wide missionary task, and minimize the differences between "home missions" and "foreign missions." Indeed, the Home Mission Societies of the American Baptist Convention and the Home Mission Board of the Southern Baptist Convention actually conduct work in some countries outside the United States, so no precise line of distinction can be drawn. The missionaries themselves have rightly led in the effort to deglamorize their special kind of work and to place themselves in the context of our general responsibility to preach the gospel to every creature, wherever the opportunity may appear. We endorse this approach because it underlines the equal urgency of our labors in New York City, India, Brazil, or wherever there are those who have not heard the word of life. There is the danger, of course, that such an emphasis may enable us to avoid the difficult and forbidding kinds of work, under protection of the argument that in the more comfortable place we are still sharing in the labors of the person who goes into hardship, danger, and loneliness in a foreign country.

Deeds of heroism and lives of hardship in the missionary enterprise are not unknown today. The perils endured by those who have remained at their posts in the world's trouble spots, in Japan, China, the Philippines, Korea, and the Congo, forbid us to become complacent about the nature of the missionary calling. Dr. William Wallace, Baptist medical missionary to China, was imprisoned and then killed after the Communists took over his mission station.

Each of the mission boards or societies under our various denominational organizations has its own organization and its own way of working. Although, in keeping with our freedom, no single pattern of intercongregational organization can be considered normative, we may take one, the Foreign Mission Board of the Southern Baptist Convention, as fairly typical. Under the appointment of the Board, and supported by Southern Baptists, missionaries are at work in eight African countries, six European countries, and four countries in the Near East. In the Latin American area, they serve in fourteen different countries, and in the Orient, in twelve. For the support of this work, in 1961 Southern Baptists gave more than $17 million, about 58 percent of the total budget for the Convention's work. A little more than half of this came through the week-by-week gifts to the churches, shared according to the vote of the churches through the Cooperative Program, which we have already described. The rest was given in special offerings. This money was used to support 1,548 missionaries who were under appointment at the end of 1961, almost equally divided among the three general areas, and to maintain hospitals and clinics, to build churches, and to operate schools, publishing centers, orphanages, and good will centers.

The work of home mission boards and societies is similar, except that their energies are directed to specialized areas of need in the homeland. City and mountain missions, work among Indians, minority groups, and foreign language groups, ministries to refugees, and liaison with institutional and military chaplains are some of the most prominent aspects of our home mission work.

In both of these general aspects of missionary work conducted by Baptists, the ministry to physical need is significant. Indeed, missions and works of mercy cannot rightly be separated. We serve and witness in the name of One who had compassion upon those who were sick, hungry, or oppressed. The ways of giving a cup of cold water in His Name have multiplied with our advancing technical knowledge and medical skill. In spite of the affluence of our American society in general, there are segments of our own population still deprived of basic necessities, and this general abundance is still unknown in large parts of today's world. We cannot substitute the ministry to physical need for the preaching of the Gospel, nor may we use such an opportunity unfairly to induce people to accept our religious views; but we may—indeed, we must—recognize that need as part of the external call to missionary service. Early in the history of the modern missionary movement, far-seeing leaders saw the need for medical missions. Since that time the vision of opportunity has been enlarged, and men and women are employing a wide diversity of gifts in missionary service all over the world. Among them are architects, agricultural engineers, journalists, medical technicians, printers, and accountants. The appearance of government-sponsored programs of aid in underdeveloped countries has not ended the need or the opportunity for our missionary ministries in such areas.

The opportunities for service in church-related institutions at home are equally varied. Our people who, for one reason or another, cannot go to a foreign land to serve, still may be missionaries. Indeed, in every land where Baptists are at work today, the concern for people in need finds expression as the "younger churches" take up their own responsibility in "home and foreign missions." There are children's homes, homes for the aged, hospitals, clinics, and convalescent homes which owe their founding and their present support to various Baptist agencies.

Institutions like these demand a great variety of skills. In them are many people who are consciously fulfilling a ministry to which they have been called in the context of their Christian experience, even though we may not usually speak of them as ministers of the gospel. By extension of their services, too, these institutions perform an even more widely varied ministry than their titles might indicate. For example, in connection with some of our hospitals, we have medical schools and schools of nursing. Others do extensive out-patient clinical work. In several there are accredited programs for training ministers in pastoral care of the sick.

As in the programs of evangelism, so here statistics might be cited to describe the scope of Baptist work and achievement. In both instances, these figures would be only a feeble and almost irrelevant gesture toward describing the accomplishments. We are dealing with immeasurable need of human lives, which are of infinite worth. However much we give, and however much we do, our efforts are still insufficient for the need, and their cost is not to be compared with the benefits received in rescue, comfort, and healing.

Baptists do not have a uniform pattern of establishing and supporting these institutions of mercy. Some of them are operated by the larger denominational bodies, such as national Baptist unions, federations, or conventions. Others are operated by local associations or by corporations formed for this special purpose. Some are jointly owned by two or more conventions or associations.

Whatever the nature of the institution, and whatever the relationship to the denomination, our institutions of mercy may well describe their function in terms quoted in the 1962 Southern Baptist Convention *Annual:*

> A Baptist hospital exists to bring men into a saving relationship with God through faith in Jesus Christ by means of a direct personal witness as occasion presents, and by a positive Christian interpretation of the experiences of disease, disability, and death . . . functions as an instrument of God's grace in enriching and prolonging human life within the scope of Divine Providence . . . enlists and teaches those called to the healing arts, encourages their maximum development in talent and skill, and provides the setting within which these may be performed as ministries of the highest order . . . makes available the full resources of the hospital

to those people least able to pay, in such ways as to preserve human dignity and worth.

Such ideals are thoroughly consonant with the Christian way as Baptists understand it, and represent a few of the many ways in which we do the work to which we are called by God's gracious and sovereign will.

PART IV

BAPTIST CONTRIBUTIONS
to the CHRISTIAN WORLD

INTRODUCTION

However varied our individual vocations as Christians may be, these are combined in a corporate calling for the whole Church, to be the body of Christ. Before concluding our study of the Baptist way of life, it is in order to ask, "What have Baptists done, and what are they doing, to contribute to the life and work of the whole body of Christ?"

John Bunyan once commented on the mutual support experienced within the Christian fellowship thus:

> Christians are like the several flowers in a garden that have upon each of them the dew of heaven, which, being shaken with the wind, they let fall at each other's roots, whereby they are jointly nourished and become nourishers of each other.

Some of our contributions have already been noted in the preceding chapters. We may dare to hope that our stress upon the Christian experience, our congregational polity, and our understanding of the ordinances may help to illumine aspects of the gospel which, be it freely confessed, is beyond the apprehension of any one of us, or even of all of us together.

The most important contribution which can be made by any religious group cannot be confined to concepts, doctrines, or patterns of organization. It is, instead, a personal contribution, made by the lives of devout men and women whose characters exemplify faith, compassion, and selflessness. If our judgment were less easily swayed by prominence, we might see that multitudes of obscure people, scarcely known beyond their own communities, have made much larger gifts to the treasury of the Church Universal than have their famous compatriots. We all have known such Christians. They continue to exert a wholesome influence in the lives of others whom they have touched. And, be they famous or quite unknown, if their apprehension of the Christian Gospel through the Baptist way has enabled them in vision, concern, or influence, to transcend the boundaries of our denomination, we may gladly let such lives be our Baptist gift to Christendom at large.

It remains for us, however, to indicate some of the ways by which our people have given expression to the truths of the Gospel, ways which have not been treated in the preceding chapters.

THEOLOGY

In the strictest sense, "theology" has to do with the doctrine of God. As such, it is only a part of the whole body of Christian teaching. Other parts are Christology (doctrinal teaching about Jesus Christ), ecclesiology (the doctrine of the church), and anthropology (the doctrine of man, understood in relation to God). More commonly, however, the word is used to designate the whole body of doctrine, or the church's explication of the whole of Christian truth. There is even a third sense, much broader yet. The word is sometimes employed to speak of the whole range of religion, or of the study of religion in all its aspects. "Theological education" involves the study of much more than "theology" alone!

We use the term here in the middle sense. By "theology" we mean the interpretation of the body of Christian truth. Let it be remembered that theology is *not* the *truth* itself, but is rather a human attempt to explain in connected and coherent fashion the truth of God's self-revelation. It is subject to error, as is all the work of fallible men. It changes; indeed, it must change. Theology reflects the changing times, with the developing language, new concepts, fresh expressions of hope, and altered views of the world. To refuse to let theology move with the moving years is to enslave it to the past. The result is then that the church has to preach another generation's gospel. We may find ourselves talking about the experience of first century men in the language of fifth century men as translated by eighteenth century men. We may not be able to claim either the experience or the language as our own, and we may be unable to communicate with our twentieth century neighbors.

Theology, then, is important for every Christian—as important as language can be. But because it is a description of God's work, a testimony, and not God's work itself, theology is not, for Baptists, the bond of unity. Our unity is rather to be found in God's revelation to man, which includes a call to man, to which man *responsibly responds* in faith.

We begin theologizing, of course, when we speak of the Christian experience even as briefly as we have done in these few sentences. But the form which we have used here is not final or authoritative. It is not binding upon Baptists. It has that same partial and transient character which belongs to all theology.

BAPTISTS AND CREEDS

It is often said that Baptists have no creed but the New Testament. In one sense this is true. There is no one statement of belief to which all Baptists subscribe, none to which one must agree in order to claim for himself the name of Baptist. We have no creedal declaration comparable to the Lutherans' Augsburg Confession, the Presbyterians' Westminster Confession, or the Thirty-nine Articles of the Church of England. Our churches generally do not recite the classic creeds of the early church, though Baptists could assent to almost all that is contained in them.

It is not true, however, that we do not have creeds. We have them, and some of them are widely used and have exerted a great influence. They are commonly called "confessions of faith." They bear witness that the Christian message as set forth in the Bible needs interpreting, and thus they declare that Baptists do not consider theology unimportant.

Nevertheless, we have contended, and still contend, that to use a manmade creed as a test of fellowship or as a disciplinary instrument would be a dangerous thing, and that it is better to endure teachings that we may dislike than for one man to sit in judgment upon another man's faith. The rejection of creeds in this sense is in clear agreement with the principle of responsible membership, which we described in the introduction to Part III. If all believers are priests, and if the way to the divine presence is open to every man, then no man's formulation of the faith is adequate for any other man, or, at any rate, it must not be made binding upon any other man.

Hence these confessions of faith are indications of the beliefs of a group of Baptists at a particular point in time, gathered in a single place. They do not speak for all Baptists, not even for all of a particular branch of our Baptist family. The Separate Baptists, who arose in America after the Great Awakening of the 1740's, generally rejected any use of confessions of faith. They feared that any such use would be a step in the direction of formalism in worship, and that it might be a step toward coercion in matters of belief. When, in 1783, the Virginia Separate Baptists adopted the Philadelphia Confession, they made it plain that their vote should:

> . . . not mean that every person is to be bound to the strict observance of everything therein contained, nor do we mean to make it, in any respect, superior or equal to the scrip-

tures in matters of faith and practice: although we think it the best composition of the kind now extant . . .[1]

The reader who is interested in pursuing the study of the confessional statements of Baptists is referred to W. L. Lumpkin's *Baptist Confessions of Faith* for an introduction to most of them and the text of several major ones. They are significant elements of primary source material for the study of Baptist theology, but they are dependable indices of this theology only when one remembers the limitations upon their authority.

GENERAL CHARACTERISTICS OF BAPTIST THEOLOGY

Early English Baptists arose in two quite distinct streams of thought and action, though both streams had their origin in the broad land called Puritanism. These two beginning groups, General Baptists and Particular Baptists, held to differing theological emphases. The General Baptists were Arminian in doctrine. That is, they taught a doctrine of general atonement and stressed man's freedom of choice. The Particular Baptists, on the other hand, believed in a limited or particular atonement, for the elect only, and so heavily stressed the sovereignty of God that they minimized man's part in the redemptive experience.

The Particular Baptists proved to be the stronger group, and through the latter part of the seventeenth century they came to overshadow the General Baptists in numbers and in influence. During the eighteenth and nineteenth centuries, both in England and in America, the dominant Baptist theology was strongly Calvinistic. Yet, those of the Arminian persuasion did not disappear, and the identity of a Baptist group

[1] *Quoted by* Albert Henry Newman, A *History of the Baptist Churches in the United States,* Sixth Edition, Revised and Enlarged (New York: Charles Scribner's Sons, 1915), p. 301.

grounded specifically in this theological outlook is preserved today in the Free Will Baptists and the General Baptists.

At the same time, those who have descended from the Particular Baptists (though no longer known by this name) have moved slowly toward the Arminian or General Baptist position. If the points of doctrine which traditionally separate Arminians from the stricter Calvinists were set before a group of one hundred Baptists, chosen at random from among the churches of the American Baptist Convention or the Southern Baptist Convention, the majority of them would agree with the Arminians on all points save one. That one is the question of apostasy, or the possibility of "falling from grace." On this point, most of our people, apart from the Free Will and General Baptist groups, probably would still hold to the Calvinist view that denies such a possibility.

On the major points of doctrine, Baptists are in harmony with the rest of the Christian world. The decisions of the early church councils on the Trinity and on the person of Christ are not questioned by most Baptists. The main stream of Baptist thought has not diverged from the interpretation of man as sinner as expounded by the Apostle Paul and elucidated by Augustine, with additions by Luther and Calvin. One may hear Anselm's doctrine of the atonement, as well as his arguments for the existence of God, preached from Baptist pulpits.

When the London Confession of 1677 was drawn up, the authors took note of the Westminster Confession and the Savoy Confession (a Congregational statement based on that of Westminster), and called attention to the agreement, "for the most part without any variation of the terms," between those two. Then they proceeded to their own task:

> . . . we did in like manner conclude it best to follow their example, in making use of the very same words with them both, in those articles (which are very many) wherein our faith and doctrine is the same with theirs. And this we

did, the more abundantly to manifest our consent with both, in all the fundamental articles of the Christian religion, as also with many others whose orthodox confessions have been published to the World, on the behalf of the protestants in diverse nations and cities; and also to convince all that we have no itch to clog religion with new words, but to readily acquiesce in that form of sound words which hath been, in consent with the holy scriptures, used by others before us; hereby declaring before God, angels, and men, our hearty agreement with them, in that wholesome protestant doctrine, which, with so clear evidence of scriptures they have asserted.[2]

This agreement with the whole Christian world, and with Protestantism in particular, may be said to be the most important single mark of Baptist theology.

At the same time, within the context of this tradition, we have placed our heaviest theological emphasis upon those doctrines which are most closely related to experiential religion. Such themes as the nature of man and his predicament; the character of faith, repentance, obedience, and assurance; God's call to man; the meaning of salvation, and the theological bases of behavior for the Christian have occupied a major part of our attention. We have been content, on the other hand, to let others lead the way in formulating Trinitarian and Christological ideas, as well as the doctrines of creation, providence, revelation, and inspiration.

BAPTIST THEOLOGICAL CONTRIBUTIONS

It may be asked why Baptists have not made a contribution to the world of theological thought in proportion to our numerical strength and our vigor in evangelism, education, and missions. We must concede that this is a true judgment and a proper question. Although we shall mention some who have made such a contribution, we cannot list a great number

[2] *Quoted by* Lumpkin, *op. cit.,* p. 245.

of theologians whose influence goes beyond the boundaries of our own denomination. The reasons for this have not been fully investigated, but some of them are quite clear.

1. First we may cite the general agreement with Protestant theology, to which we have already alluded. Baptists have not felt a compulsion to write systematic theologies, for example, because we have been able to use those produced in the context of other churches. There is no distinctive Baptist doctrine of God. We do not differ with the Methodists in Christology, nor with Lutherans in Trinitarian faith, nor with Presbyterians in the doctrine of man. Hence, in a course in systematic theology, a student in a Baptist seminary will be likely to read, and to use as textbooks, the works of Methodist, Lutheran, and Reformed theologians. Our distinctive beliefs do not require us to rewrite the whole "body of divinity" from our own perspective.

2. A second reason is suggested by our history as a denomination. A large part of our life has been lived out on the frontier. Here in America, in particular, we have been a frontier people for most of our years. The energies of our people have been turned to tasks other than the formulation of theology, and we have not had a long life as a mature and settled denomination. Vitality and reflective thought are not necessarily opposed to each other; evangelism and scholarship are not mutually exclusive. Yet, a group may abound in one and neglect the other, and this has been true of Baptists all too often. The result has been, on occasion, an evangelism not firmly grounded in theological truth or Biblical insight. We may be reaching a level of maturity and adjustment that will enable us now to give our attention to theological tasks.

3. A third reason for our lack of theological productivity is a rather widespread suspicion of education and of educated men. Happily this has already disappeared in many places; but elsewhere Baptists are still the frontier folk to whom a high de-

gree of education spells death to evangelistic zeal, and accomplishments in scholarship are incompatible with heartfelt religion and deep spiritual insight. For this reason our men who have been capable of writing have been discouraged from doing so. When they have ventured to appear in print they have been subjected to the criticism of their own people. While we recognize the importance of research and writing among professors in other fields in our Baptist schools, we are generally willing for theological professors simply to reflect popular theological opinions rather than to think and write creatively or to provide leadership in the fields of their competence. This is not equally true among all Baptists, of course, but it still is a strong enough factor to account for some of our failure to contribute our share to the theological treasury of the church.

4. Still another reason for our lack in this respect may be our own Baptist self-understanding. It has been suggested by some perceptive students that in a large part of the Baptist fellowship this self-interpretation is shallow and defective. We acknowledge our kinship with other Protestants on the great central themes of the Christian message about God, man, Christ, atonement, and forgiveness of sins. We proceed then to think that our distinctiveness is not in any sense theological, but rather only programmatic, or functional. That is, we may be inclined to think of ourselves as people who simply have a different way of doing things, a better program, a more efficient organization, than others enjoy. Wherever this is our self-understanding, there is little incentive for solid and creative theological study or writing.

We acknowledge our failures in our theological responsibility to the Christian world. Yet, it would be incorrect and unjust to leave the impressions that Baptists have done no theological thinking or writing. Early English Baptists were vigorous pamphleteers in the twin causes of reformation and religious liberty. Almost without exception these pamphlets were based upon theological considerations and not merely upon a political or social ideal or concept of liberty.

In more recent times, the work of such men as Andrew Fuller of England has helped to soften the older Calvinism and to provide a theological basis for Christian missions.

Baptists probably have made their greatest contribution to the theological world, both in terms of creativity and in terms of the total bulk of work, in various aspects of Biblical study. This is to be expected from a people so profoundly concerned with loyalty to the Scriptures. The name of A. T. Robertson is known wherever the Greek New Testament is studied. His "Big Grammar," over which seminarians have toiled for uncounted hours, is still an important work almost fifty years after its publication. In Old Testament studies, H. Wheeler Robinson is perhaps the best known Baptist contributor. His successors in the English Baptist tradition are keeping up a lively and progressive study of the Old Testament today. T. R. Glover, another English Baptist, was professor and public orator at Cambridge, where he used his wealth of classical knowledge in the interpretation of the New Testament world.

One of the most able historians yet to appear among Baptists is A. H. Newman, who wrote on the general history of the Christian movement as well as on Baptist history. Still active as interpreter of Christian missions and historian of the Christian enterprise is Kenneth Scott Latourette, who deserves to be mentioned as missionary statesman as well.

The influence of Walter Rauschenbusch, a German-American Baptist, upon Christianity in America through the Social Gospel movement, is beyond all calculation. He combined a warm and vital personal religion with a keen sense of the social aspects of the church's mission, and his burning zeal for social righteousness lighted fires of concern in almost every denomination. Shailer Mathews, one-time president of the

Northern (now American) Baptist Convention, is another of our company who shared significantly in this field of labor.

These names will suffice to indicate the wide diversity of gifts which our Baptist people have contributed to theological study. They should help to clear us of the charge that we are without any theological orientation. Others, as we shall note in the next chapter, have ably interpreted the gospel through other forms of religious literature which, while not formally theological, nevertheless have meaning for interpreting the will of God for human life.

How many Baptists make a contribution to Christian theology today? It is fair to expect that, as we become more mature as a denomination, we shall have opportunity, as well as obligation, to share our peculiar insights into the Christian message with the rest of the world. If we do this in a spirit of pride, our offerings will properly be rejected. But if, without apology and with proper humility, we seek to enter into conversation with our Christian brothers, we may be able to speak a significant message to the whole Christian community. In order to achieve this, we must first of all recognize and study the theological basis of our existence as a distinct part of the world-wide family of Christian believers. This means that we are obliged to concentrate special attention upon the profession that we follow the New Testament pattern of church order and teaching.

Of this position, this intention, Baptists are not ashamed, and would sooner give up our name, our organizational forms, even our hard-won gains in religious liberty, than yield this adherence to the Bible. For with this we could begin again. The first article of the London Confession of 1677 offers what is perhaps the most detailed and most eloquent statement of a Baptist view of Scripture. It deserves quoting at some length, because it helps to describe our stance, and it suggests something of what we have to offer to the Christian world:

1. The Holy Scripture is the only sufficient, certain, and infallible rule of all saving Knowledge, Faith, and Obedience. . . .

5. We may be moved and induced by the testimony of the Church of God, to an high and reverent esteem of the Holy Scriptures; . . . yet, notwithstanding; our full perswasion, and assurance of the infallible truth, and divine authority thereof, is from the inward work of the Holy Spirit, bearing witness by and with the Word in our Hearts.

6. The whole Councel of God concerning all things necessary for his own Glory, Mans Salvation, Faith and Life, is either expressely set down or necessarily contained in the Holy Scripture; unto which nothing at any time is to be added, whether by new Revelation of the Spirit, or traditions of men.

Nevertheless we acknowledge the inward illumination of the Spirit of God, to be necessary for the saving understanding of such things as are revealed in the Word. . . .

10. The supream judge by which all controversies of Religion are to be determined, and all Decrees of Councels, opinions of antient Writers, Doctrines of men, and private Spirits, are to be examined, and in whose sentence we are to rest, can be no other but the Holy Scripture delivered by the Spirit, into which Scripture so delivered, our faith is finally resolved.[3]

There are signs that Baptists are developing a new interest in the whole message of the Bible. Consequently, it appears that we have our best opportunity to make a real contribution to the Christian world in the realm of Biblical study. We share the opinion of John Robinson, Separatist pastor of a group of English exiles in Holland, who believed that "God hath yet more light and truth to break forth out of his Holy Word." As we develop a larger number of able and well-trained Biblical scholars, who are not afraid to grapple with the most difficult and critical problems of interpretation, we would be

[3] *Quoted by* Lumpkin, *op. cit.*, pp. 248, 250, 252.

able to place in the common treasury of the Christian world our proportionate share of insights into the truth of Holy Scripture.

It is to be hoped that we shall share with the rest of Christendom also our Baptist understanding of the Church and its ordinances. Already there is evidence that Baptists are participating in the recently-renewed discussion centering on these topics and involving Christians of every communion.

It may be that the doctrine of the church is the most vigorously discussed of all theological topics today. Such books as Robert Walton's *The Gathered Community; Baptist Concepts of the Church,* edited by Winthrop S. Hudson; and *What is the Church?,* edited by Duke K. McCall, will introduce the reader to some of the current discussion. We may hope that this conversation will continue and will be enlarged so as to involve further exchanges of understanding with non-Baptist theologians. Such conversations, carried on in a spirit of mutual respect and trust, can only result in enrichment and deeper appreciation of the many-sided Christian heritage.

Baptists should be able to make a contribution to the theology of evangelism as well. We have always been insistent upon evangelism as a primary reason for the very existence of the church, and this contention should not be given up. There is evidence, however, that our people are not satisfied with the current quality of evangelism, and that a real effort is being made to ground our preaching of the good news in a sound and wholesome theology. This is great gain, and it will be an even greater gain if we can combine evangelistic zeal with a more adequate theology. We need not become less vitally concerned with the spiritual welfare of men, or less eager to win them to faith in Christ. We do need to examine the basis of our concern and to support this eagerness with understanding of the dynamics of conversion and the religious experience. We need to undergird our programs of evangelism with a doctrine of God that is compatible with the Christian faith, with a clear and Biblical understanding of man as sinner, and with a view of the Christian life which takes the commitment of self to God in faith with utmost seriousness.

Finally, we may hope that increasing breadth and depth of scholarship will enable Baptists to take their place among others in the front line of general theological advance. Not all the work in any theological realm has yet been done. The fact that we can accept and use the work of a Lutheran theologian like Gustaf Aulen on the atonement, or of a Reformed theologian like Emil Brunner on revelation, does not release us from the obligation to devote serious and sustained thought to the problems attending these themes of Christian doctrine. If we take seriously the principle of stewardship, we must confess a responsibility to exercise our talents in these areas of thought and to share our insights with other Christians. Baptists of other days, such as John Gill, Andrew Fuller, John Leadley Dagg, A. H. Strong, James P. Boyce, and E. Y. Mullins have offered creative theological leadership, and we have no need to be ashamed of their work. It will not suffice, however, for our own responsibility to the Christian world of the latter part of the twentieth century. That responsibility is urgent, inescapable, ecumenical, and theological.

CONTROVERSIES
in the LIFE of BAPTISTS

The occurrence of not-infrequent controversies in Baptist life has caused concern and chagrin among the lovers of peace. Such disputes always tend to bring out unlovely traits in the antagonists. The whole Christian cause suffers from schisms. We Baptists have our share of those disputatious souls who "love a good fight"; but the controversies marking Baptist life cannot be explained altogether in terms of a contentious spirit. This discussion is not written in order to justify us in our quarrels. It does, however, frankly acknowledge that controversy has been a part of our story, and it offers some explanations as to the origin and frequency of these family disputes in which we have engaged.

In each of the discussions there are intrinsic issues, which are as complex as in any dispute in political, theological, or ecclesiological communities. Apart from these, however, there are certain factors in Baptist life which, when properly recognized, may help to make the course of events more readily understandable. To these factors we now call attention.

1. In the first place, we risk saying the too-obvious by remarking that these controversies have to do with matters which Baptists take seriously. They are not cases of "much ado about nothing," at least from the Baptist viewpoint. Indeed, it may be said that the very fact that such disputes do arise is in itself a declaration that Baptists take their religion seriously enough to fight among themselves over its interpretation and its institutional expression. In a sense, then, they are a testimony to the same vitality which finds more commendable expression in some other forms. Though we deplore the divisive spirit that fosters and is fostered by such disagreements, we cannot fail to rejoice in the intensity with which our Baptist people approach even their disagreements. Such storms may be preferable to peaceful lethargy and total indifference.

2. Another partial explanation of these controversies is that they are a kind of growing pain. We are still a young denomination. Several of our family disputes have arisen in the frontier situations as we were working out problems created by a totally new environment. Baptists have always attempted to unite the basic pattern of the New Testament churches with a polity suited to the modern age. This means that we continue to be a young church, continually seeking the structure through which best to express the Christian gospel and the insights given to us in its interpretation. Our perpetual "immaturity" probably promises still more of the same history of controversy so long as our present course of development continues.

3. A more obvious kind of growth, bringing its own attendant problems, is our numerical increase. At some stages in Baptist life, the denomination has experienced rapid growth in membership. Sometimes this has been far too rapid to allow complete assimilation of the new members into the life and

traditions of the churches. In some instances, a period of spectacular revival has brought an influx of members to the churches, and soon thereafter controversy has ensued.

Leaders in the early Church foresaw some of the problems in this kind of situation, and they wisely provided for pre-baptismal instruction through the use of catechisms. Baptists generally have not used this method of training new members, though Baptist catechisms have been written. Our churches in increasing numbers are giving some guidance to young converts through a "pastor's class," or some other program of teaching, but this still is not common enough. Even our massive efforts at training members after baptism fall short. In the Southern Baptist Convention, for example, the Baptist Training Union, which has as its avowed purpose "Training in Church Membership," reaches only a fraction of the total membership. Some of our disruptive disagreements could be avoided if our people were more fully oriented to the total Christian world and to our Baptist heritage in particular. Failure to meet this challenge may mean still more unhappy division within the fellowship.

4. A fourth factor that may help to account for lively disagreement among Baptists is the very structure in which we live and work. The liberties enjoyed in a free church pattern and the principle of voluntary association carry certain risks. Among these is the risk that two people, or two groups of people, who find themselves in agreement and who, therefore, extend recognition to each other, in another context or in an issue which does not at first appear may discover that they operate upon quite different presuppositions. Without a body of definitely stated beliefs, agreed upon in advance as to substance, limits, and authority, such a discovery may issue in sharp disagreement and even division.

It may appear to the non-Baptist that our disagreements in the past few years portend a total disintegration of our fellowship. This is surely too pessimistic a view. Although the quarrels within our family are more widely publicized than formerly, they probably are no more severe than the less well-known disputes of earlier days. Some of these have resulted in the separation of groups who dissented from the views and policies of the majority. While we deplore such separation, we must still concede the right of those who can no longer conscientiously work within the framework of the denomination's polity. The Southern Baptist Convention was formed as a result of this kind of disagreement in 1845, when (as previously pointed out) the mission board of the old Triennial Convention refused to appoint a slaveholder as a missionary. In recent years both the American Baptist Convention and the Southern Baptist Convention have experienced losses in the withdrawal of some who saw in these conventions certain trends toward "liberalism" which they could not condone. Others have separated themselves because of disagreements over denominational organization and polity.

It may be argued that the disagreements themselves are not destructive. Within a free church context, new insights and new bases for further agreement may be hammered out in the clear statement of divergent opinions and the charitable discussion of these divergences. In 1888, John Clifford, pastor in London, came to the presidency of the British Baptist Union in the midst of theological unrest and criticism. Some members of the Union feared the results of Biblical criticism which others were undertaking. The controversy engendered by these fears disturbed still others. In his presidential address on "The Great Forty Years," Clifford sought to allay the distress and to suggest that positive results might ensue from the disagreements.

> Study of the ages of controversy ought to quiet our alarm, enlarge patience, extirpate self-seeking, exclude personal recriminations, exalt brotherly love, quicken joyful trust in, and large expectancy from, the Gracious Ruler of His Church. . . .

Controversy is far better than stagnation. Even strife is a sign of vitality—uncomfortable, irritating vitality, perhaps; exceedingly disagreeable to fossil theologians and actual tyrants; but still it is a vitality, and one of the various forms of that law of the struggle for existence which runs into the realm of ideas and of spirit. . . .

Even the first friends of Christianity were never agreed as to its whole contents. Living men differ. It is the dead who agree. Poor shattered fragments that we are! Why! truth would have no chance at all upon the earth if each man were nothing but the sibilant echo of his fellow. God sets men at different angles to the truth, so that one may see what others cannot, and, thereby, more of her virginal beauty and perennial loveliness be revealed to men. . . .

God will not suffer us to get our best beliefs as we do our coats. . . . Give men a ready-made faith, paid for by pen subscription, or lip affirmation, and it is on them, not in them; on them like a garment, not in them as a life.

Give us a Bible about which two opinions are not possible, and we treat it as we do the multiplication table, use it for our grossest needs; but never think of it for the splendid hours of spiritual aspiration and redeeming service.[1]

It is evident that not all of us can view disagreement, theological or ecclesiastical, with such equanimity. Yet, in the presence of a common religious experience, a common love of God, and a common task, surely the Baptist fellowship may endure the stresses of disagreement and come through the experience with added wisdom and new strength.

[1] Quoted from A *Baptist Treasury*, edited by Sydnor L. Stealey (New York: Thomas Y. Crowell Company, 1958), pp. 97-102.

HYMNODY and OTHER
RELIGIOUS LITERATURE

If Baptists were to be called upon to settle up accounts in terms of what we have received from the rest of the Christian world in hymnody and devotional literature, and what we have given in return, some surprises might be in store for both parties to the transaction. We should surely find ourselves still in debt after the accounting ended, for we have received more than we have given; but we would not need to be ashamed of the quality of some of our contributions to the treasures of the Christian world. Fortunately, it is not required of us that we measure out line for line and note for note. Such a debt as we owe is at least partially paid as soon as it is acknowledged, and another installment is paid whenever we seek worthily to use that which we have received from our fellow-Christians.

We gladly acknowledge our debt to those of other denominations for their hymns which we sing and enjoy, their prayers which inspire us, and their meditations which disturb and enrich our lives. On any Sunday in the year, one may hear in a Baptist church the words of devotion and praise from the pen of Martin Luther, Isaac Watts, Augustus Toplady, and Phillips Brooks. We sing the songs of the Methodists' Charles Wesley, of Reginald Heber of the Anglican communion, and of Cardinal Newman of the Roman Catholic Church. In this respect, perhaps more than in any other, Baptists, along with other Protestants, are constantly and genuinely ecumenical. We recognize that, in spite of confessional and ecclesiastical differences that separate us, we enjoy a unity, at a profound level of life and worship, with others who acknowledge Jesus Christ as Lord.

CHRISTIAN HYMNODY

Hymn-singing is an integral part of Protestant worship to-day in almost every setting. It is difficult, therefore, for us to picture that time when it was strenuously opposed, and its practice was sufficient reason for some Christians to withdraw fellowship from others. Yet, so it was in the seventeenth century, among the English churches. The tradition of congregational singing of hymns, known in the early Church and among Continental Protestants, was overshadowed by the tradition of using only the Psalms, in a metrical version. The influence of Calvinism in Great Britain confirmed this attitude.

Various arguments were advanced against the use of hymns. They were "articles of human composure," not, like the Psalms, divinely inspired. Some Protestants, on the other hand, believed that the free influence of the Spirit of God might be stifled by the use of "some set stinted form," like that of the hymns. Others feared that no direct Scriptural basis for congregational singing could be found, especially since the hymns might be sung by "mixed multitudes," by "professors and prophane alike" (*i.e.*, by those who "professed" faith in Christ in unseemly union with unbelievers).

Isaac Watts is usually called "the father of English hymnody." It is true that he, more than any other single person, is responsible for the development of hymns that combine literary excellence and religious truth. Yet, before Watts' first book of hymns was published, some Baptists in England had published their own efforts in this field and were establishing the practice of congregational hymn-singing in their churches.

Abraham Cheare was one of these. In 1672 he issued "A Looking Glass for Children," containing a number of children's hymns of his own composition. Still more significant was the work of Benjamin Keach, pastor of a Baptist chapel in Southwark. He, too, wrote hymns for children, but his chief accomplishment was that of leading his people to accept congregational singing as a regular part of worship. To this end he wrote hymns week by week to accompany his sermons, although it was twenty years after he began his effort before his church accepted their use as a regular thing.

Keach's ability as poet and hymn-writer was limited, and all his hymns have long since ceased to be used. They cannot compare in quality with the work of Watts, nor with that of some later Baptist writers. Nevertheless, his *Spiritual Melody*, published in 1691, deserves recognition as a pioneering work, and it no doubt helped to make the way easier for the acceptance of Watt's more promising work a few years later.

As a rule, the General Baptists of this time strongly opposed hymn-singing. Among the Particular Baptists opinion was divided. Before the end of the seventeenth century, associations were solemnly considering in their gatherings the serious query, "Whether singing the praises of God by the whole church in their public assemblies be a gospel duty, or not?"

Happily, Keach and some other supporters of the practice were able to advance a strong Scriptural argument in their support. They pointed to the report in the Gospel that, after the Last Supper, Jesus and his disciples sang a hymn before they left the upper room. By placing the hymn at the close of the service, they maintained the Biblical pattern, and at the same time they made it convenient for dissenters to leave the service if their consciences so required. One of the associations recognized the practice in the following fashion:

> Whereas several of our members are satisfied in their judgment concerning singing an hymn after the Lord's Supper, we declare that we are willing our brethren and sisters so satisfied should enjoy the liberty of their conscience in the matter, provided it be performed in this order, *viz.*, after the ordinance of the Lord's Supper is concluded, praises to God by our prayer and contributions made and all other business belonging to the church ended. That then those who in their judgment are for singing an hymn may stay and so sing without any offence to those who are not satisfied in the practice. And we, on the other hand, declare we will not be offended with any of our brethren and sisters who have not freedom and satisfaction to join with us therein, nor be present while so doing.

This kind of concession, however, did not prevent a schism in Keach's church. Twenty-two members left to form another congregation because they could not condone the practice of congregational singing.

Although the listing of names and hymns in our present context can only be a token of the total Baptist contribution, it may be enlightening to show something of the variety of hymns written by our people. Some would include John Bunyan in the list, though his connection with the Baptists was not permanent, and though his hymn-writing was incidental and not nearly so significant as his other contributions to the Christian world. We are on firmer ground when we cite the work of Miss Anne Steele, who has been called one of the ablest followers of the Isaac Watts tradition of hymn-writing, even though few of her hymns are sung today. Better known are Robert Robinson's "Come, Thou Fount of Every Blessing" and "Mighty God, While Angels Bless Thee." Samuel Medley, Baptist pastor in Liverpool, wrote "Awake, My Soul." We owe two well-known hymns to Samuel Stennett: "Majestic Sweetness Sits Enthroned" and "On Jordan's Stormy Banks I Stand." Edward Mote, author of "My Hope is Built on Nothing Less," was a nineteenth century British Baptist pastor.

John Fawcett, pastor at Wainsgate, wrote "Blest Be the Tie that Binds our Hearts." An unverified story tells that in 1772 he was called to a pastorate in London. After he had preached his farewell sermon and his furniture was loaded on the wagons for departure, the grief of his people in Wainsgate so moved him that he changed his mind and decided to stay with them, even though they were never to pay more than twenty-five pounds a year for his support.

The authorship of "How Firm a Foundation" has never been precisely determined, though it is generally ascribed now to Robert Keene, member of the Carter Lane Baptist congregation in London. This hymn first appears in a collection issued by John Rippon, another Baptist, in 1787, marked only with the initial "K_____."

American Baptists have also contributed hymns of lasting merit. Samuel Francis Smith, author of "My Country, 'Tis of Thee," also wrote the missionary hymn entitled "The Morning Light is Breaking." We owe to S. Dryden Phelps the words of "Savior, Thy Dying Love." Harry Emerson Fosdick, widely known as preacher, writer, and teacher, has given us a splendid hymn, "God of Grace and God of Glory." Many modern hymnals and collections of gospel songs include several of the works of P. P. Bliss, which, although they are not of the highest literary quality, have survived for a century now as valid expressions of experiential religion.

One wonders, in going through the biographies and writings of eighteenth century Baptists, if there was a minister among them who did not write verses to be set to music. Some, like John Ryland, John Fawcett, and Benjamin Beddome, followed the example of Benjamin Keach in writing a hymn to follow and summarize each Sunday's sermon, and several collections of these were published. Most of them, of course, did not outlive their authors. Others were nothing more than pious doggerel. Yet, they were written according to a standard of literary merit different from our own, and they served purposes in their day which they could not serve today. They form a part of the contribution made by our Baptist people to the whole Christian community.

OTHER RELIGIOUS LITERATURE

In several other fields of religious literature Baptists have added to the common treasure of Christendom. Much of that issuing from the pens of seventeenth century Baptists, of course, was polemical in character, and polemical literature is rarely edifying. This literature represents not only an effort to defend Baptist principles against attack, but also an attempt to articulate, for our own use, those insights which had been gained but not yet fully formulated.

One can readily understand why the focal concern of these writings would be upon religious liberty. That governmental power should be used to coerce the minds of free men and to compel their acceptance of dogmas and patterns of church order was unthinkable, even to those Baptists who had been reared in an environment where this was accepted. Some of the most powerful writings to come from our people are concerned with this issue, and we shall note some of them in the next chapter.

Apart from this particular context of writing, however, it appears that the most effective Baptist literary witness is devoted to the explication of the Christian experience and to fostering the life of piety. For the fulfilment of these purposes, devotional literature, rather than treatises strictly theological, has been employed. The themes upon which our hymn-writers have dwelt have occupied many other writers. These have been prominent in the sermons, which, in terms of sheer bulk, constitute our largest single written contribution to the world. Much of this has an appeal only for the age and people for whom it was written.

The most remarkable form of encouragement to the Christian life from Baptist writers is that of the spiritual allegory, of which John Bunyan was the great exponent. We know him today as a writer, but he was known to his contemporaries as a preacher as well. One of his friends told of seeing a crowd of twelve hundred people gathered to hear him preach at 7:00 in the morning on a dark wintry day, and a working day at that. The world remembers him primarily for his *Pilgrim's Progress*. His lesser known works are: *The Holy War* and *Grace Abounding to the Chief of Sinners*. These also deserve to be read, not merely as examples of piety in another age, but as timeless expressions of religious truth. They show a spirit, too, that was incapable of restricted sympathies. While one can tell from reading his works that he was a Protestant, and that he held profound convictions about the character of the Christian life, it would be difficult to discern a denominational connection in most of what he wrote. Although few other allegorists had religious insights or literary gifts to equal those of Bunyan, many paid him the high compliment of imitation.

There are others among us whose work has been more specifically set within a single nation, or who have made their chief contribution by interpreting our message to the rest of the Christian world. In this number are such men as Johann Gerhard Oncken, founder of the first Baptist work in Germany; John Howard Shakespeare, secretary of the British Baptist Union, who strove valiantly to unite the Free Churches;

Alexander Carson of Ireland, and Morgan Edwards, who was born in Wales and labored in England, Ireland, and America. Through each of these, and through multitudes of others less widely known, but who nevertheless belong to the whole company of Christ's Church, inspiration and Baptist ways of understanding the Christian gospel have been shared with the rest of the world.

RELIGIOUS LIBERTY

Dominion over conscience is that part of God's empire of which he is most jealous. The imposition of a human creed is a third action, and before any man can perform it, he must do two other exploits; he must usurp the throne, and claim the slave.

Robert Robinson, English Baptist author, thus concludes a part of his *Reflections on Religious Liberty*. This is only one of a great number of writings produced by Baptists in almost every generation of our history on behalf of freedom for all men in matters of religious belief and practice.

More widely acknowledged than any of our contributions to theological understanding, church polity, or devotional literature is our continuing insistence upon religious liberty. Non-Baptist historians and statesmen have conceded that this noble concern is, and has been, in a peculiar sense a Baptist heritage.

We have been eager to possess this liberty for ourselves. The first Baptist churches arose out of a situation in which consciences were subjected to official control, and the establishment of a single religious belief and its corresponding institution was accepted as the normal, right, and orderly course of governmental action. At first glance it might appear only natural that they should seek relief from these restrictions. Who does not want to be free from the dictation of others in matters of conscience and in the exercise of his religious convictions and practices? Every martyr to the Inquisition, and every heretic in any age who has suffered exile, imprisonment, or death for his beliefs has desired this liberty for himself.

It is the distinctive Baptist contribution, however, to have sought liberty not only for ourselves but for all men, of whatever opinion. The same Robert Robinson whom we quoted above argued:

> One part of Christianity consists of propositions to be believed. Liberty to be a Christian believer is liberty to examine these propositions, to form a judgment of them, and to come to a self-determination, according to our own best abilities. Another part of Christianity consists of duties to be performed. Liberty to be a practical Christian is liberty to perform these duties, either as they regard God, our neighbor, or ourselves. Liberty to be a Christian implies liberty not to be a Christian, as liberty to examine a proposition implies liberty to reject the arguments brought to support it, if they appear inconclusive, as well as liberty to admit them, if they appear demonstrative.

This is an important aspect of religious freedom as we understand it, for there are interpretations which are far more restricted. So long as men are free only to accept an idea, a pattern of religious belief, or a way of life, and are not equally free to reject it, the consequences are that some men are free and others are not. We cannot endorse so limited a concept of freedom. It even distorts the character of that which is granted, and keeps it from being genuine liberty.

The same view is expressed by John Leland, an intrepid American Baptist fighter for freedom in the early days of our nation. He reviewed the Bill of Rights in the Massachusetts constitution in 1780, giving particular attention to the provisions concerning religion:

> "And every denomination of Christians, demeaning themselves peaceably, and as good subjects of the Commonwealth, shall be equally under the protection of the law: and no subordination of any one sect or denomination to another, shall ever be established by law." This is very liberal, to a certain degree: but if it read *all men* instead of *every denomination of Christians*, it would be unexceptionable.

Leland was not the first American Baptist to undertake the cause of religious liberty. Indeed, our history in this country begins with the work of Roger Williams, founder of the settlement of Providence, Rhode Island (where he helped to establish the first American Baptist church in 1639) and pioneer in the cause of freedom. In the settlement at Providence, where he was active in securing a charter for the colony and in formulating the civil code, absolute liberty of conscience in religious matters was assured to "papists and protestants, Jews and Turks." The summary of his *The Bloudy Tenent, of Persecution for cause of Conscience*, written in 1644, affirmed that:

> It is the will and command of God, that . . . a permission of the most Paganish, Jewish, Turkish, or Antichristian consciences and worships, bee granted to all men in all Nations and Countries: and they are onely to bee fought against with that Sword which is onely able to conquer, to wit, the Sword of Gods Spirit, the Word of God.

One of his friends and associates, Dr. John Clarke, shared Williams' beliefs in this vital area. He, too, had found the climate of opinion in Massachusetts uncongenial and had sought a place of more freedom. With the help and encouragement of the Providence company, he and some friends settled on the island of Aquidneck, which later came to be called Rhode Island. Clarke was influential in the formation of the initial compact of government, which declared that "none bee accounted Delinquent for Doctrine." Then, when Newport, Providence, and other towns came together to form the Colony of Providence Plantations, the general laws of the colony provided the same guarantees, not only for those who held the views of religion approved by the majority, but for all, so long as they did not disturb the peace or civil well-being of the community.

Liberty in religious matters was claimed for all men by these Baptists, as by our people today, not as a privilege but as a right. It is this distinction that sets off the Baptist view of religious liberty from some others that may, at first glance, resemble it. This is the reason for our insistence that the goal we seek is not religious toleration, but liberty. Our contention is more than a matter of language. The idea of toleration implies a condescension upon the part of the person or party granting the toleration. It suggests that this person or party has the right and the authority *not* to tolerate any divergence of opinion and practice, that allows any divergence through sheer generosity or because of expediency, and that it may with perfect right revoke the freedom which is enjoyed by the tolerated person or party or point of view. When this position is fully understood, it is seen to involve a separation of religious groups into two categories: the one, which occupies a favored place, enjoys that place by right; all others, although possessing liberty, do so by the permission of the favored group which, for the moment, does not choose to exercise its power to suppress dissent. This is not a halfway house on the way to true liberty, but a wholly different thing, unworthy of the name of liberty. As for the favored place for one religion, upon which this scheme of things is built, we do not claim it for ourselves, and we do not concede it to anyone else as rightful and just.

On the other hand, liberty, for which we plead, does not imply any such favored or established religion or denomination. When we affirm the right of religious liberty, we claim for ourselves and for all men that freedom which no man or group of men rightfully withholds from any other. Indeed, it is not within the province of human authority to give or to withhold, but is itself a gift of God, for which we are accountable to God alone, for "God alone is Lord of the consciences of men."

It is necessary to observe the restriction suggested here, since some have parodied our belief in liberty so that it seems to say, "It makes no difference what a man believes." This is wholly foreign to our understanding of Christian responsibility, and it does not follow by force of logic from our demand for religious liberty. What we say, instead, is that although one's beliefs do matter greatly, it is not our business to sit in judgment upon another man's beliefs, for this is to arrogate to ourselves the prerogatives of Deity.

But will not unrestricted liberty of religious opinion result in the flourishing of error? Perhaps, and we do not intend to exhibit indifference to all kinds of notions and interpretations of the Christian gospel. Some there are which we believe to be erroneous, and indeed destructive of the values which are cherished by most of Christendom. The writer of *The Ancient Bounds*, published in 1645, recognized this danger:

> I contend not for variety of opinions. I know there is but one truth; But this truth cannot be so easily brought forth without this liberty; and a generall restraint, though intended but for errours, yet through the unskilfulnesse of men, may fall upon the truth; and better many errours suffered, than one usefull truth be obstructed or destroyed.

The same Robert Robinson, whom we have already quoted, insisted that "the abuse of any blessing is no conclusive argument against the proper use of it."

Nor are we convinced that truth is so fragile, so defenseless, that it requires the coercive efforts of fallible men against other fallible men to assure its preservation and ultimate victory. To plead this point of view is to voice confidence in human wisdom and ingenuity, and to make absolute our fleeting and fragmentary glimpses of truth that towers above us all.

We Baptists are not convinced by the argument that the tradition of an established church ought to be maintained for the sake of civil order. It is not the business of the church to enforce, with spiritual sanctions, the intentions of any single form or structure of government. While urging men to be subject to lawful authority and to conduct themselves as good citizens of the commonwealth, we cannot concede that the government is justified in making of the church—of any church—its agent for the maintenance of order. We have seen that the uniting of church and state results too easily in superficial religion, a weakened sense of ethical responsibility, and a discrimination against dissenters from the established church; this situation is at best a mild persecution. At its worst this alliance results in the horrors of imprisonment and even death for the heretic.

Our insistence upon religious liberty is not merely a political ideal. It is theologically grounded. It agrees precisely with our understanding of the Reformation principle of the priesthood of all believers. One aspect of this principle is the belief that we are *inter*dependent, and that we can be, and are, priests one for another. But another, equally important, aspect is this: that no specially ordained priesthood is necessary, but that access to God is God's gift to every man. Every man is ultimately responsible to God for his acceptance or rejection of the divine will. No one can shift the burden of this responsibility to another man, nor can anyone assume it on behalf of another. Therefore, to restrict the liberty of any man in matters of religion is to remove some of the conditions necessary for the exercise of his responsibility under God. "If I am accountable to God for my response to His call, how can I fulfil my obligation in a setting where some religious opinions and practices are forbidden to me, while others are prescribed for me by human authority?"

Our Baptist understanding of the nature of faith also leads to the conclusion that religious liberty is consonant with the Christian gospel. Submission to the coercive power of the state, even when that power is exercised on behalf of an established church, is not faith. Nor is faith to be defined as the acceptance of a set of propositions which have been given legislative or royal sanction. No legislature or king on earth has the right to compel faith. Indeed, none can do so, right or no right, for that which is exacted by compulsion can never be more than acquiescence; it cannot be faith. Robert Robinson went to the heart of the matter:

> . . . the nature of faith does not admit an imposition; it signifies nothing to say, kings command it; if angels commanded it, they would require an impossibility, and exact that of me, which they themselves could not perform.

On the contrary, faith involves willing commitment and personal acceptance of the will of God. We strenuously object to any arrangement of governmental affairs or ecclesiastical structures that would seek to inhibit faith, or that would offer men a counterfeit of faith in the form of acceptance of humanly contrived opinions on religious themes and issues.

Our Baptist understanding of the nature of the church and of the state must be mentioned here, too, since they have a bearing upon the demand for freedom of religion. Baptists are not committed to any single theory of government or political philosophy. It has become habitual for our people in America to assume that democracy and the Baptist way of life are inextricably bound together, but this is not true. We may argue—and, we think, with good reason—that a democratic form of government is particularly compatible with the stress upon freedom and the worth of the individual which we Baptists cherish. At the same time, we must remember that Baptists in other parts of the world may be equally well-persuaded that a monarchy or an aristocracy offers the best government. Whatever the form of government, however, Baptists the world over generally agree that the state and the church have two different provinces of responsibility, that their constituencies are not the same, and that they possess two totally different kinds of authority. Therefore, even when their purposes coincide (as, for example, in the desire that justice be done, or that integrity in business dealings be maintained), each must seek to achieve the ends which it desires by means proper to itself. When the state becomes an agency for enforcing the church's intentions, or the church for the state's intentions, uniformity and order may be gained at the cost of liberty. Baptists are not convinced of the rightness of the medieval doctrine of the two swords, the state wielding coercive power on behalf of the church along with its own exercise of power in other matters.

This is the context of Baptist insistence upon the separation of church and state. We recognize, of course, that it is unrealistic to speak of an absolute separation. This would be possible only if the church were able to exist in a realm where no government functioned. In this case the church would be so totally withdrawn from the affairs of men that it could not at all fulfil its mission. The churches of every denomination in our country find it impossible to escape the government, even though they reject any establishment of religion. They enjoy police and fire protection provided by the government; they are subject to regulations such as building codes, and they may hold property, sue, and be sued according to the laws of the several states. When we speak of separation of church and state, we do not mean to propose that all such connections as these be abolished.

Instead, we mean to insist that the government shall exercise its authority "only in civil things," as the covenant of citizens in Providence expresses it, not in "religious concernments" wherein all men ought to have full liberty. The other side of the same conviction is that no religion ought so to be established by legal grants, advantages, or special privileges that it may direct the course of government's action or use the powers of government for the enforcement of its practices or opinions.

Leonard Busher, an English Baptist, published in 1614 an eloquent argument advancing the cause of freedom, entitled *Religions Peace: or A Plea for Liberty of Conscience.*

> Kings and magistrates are to rule temporal affairs by the swords of their temporal kingdoms, and bishops and ministers are to rule spiritual affairs by the word and Spirit of God, the sword of Christ's spiritual kingdom, and not to intermeddle one with another's authority, office, and function. . . .
>
> Therefore may it please your majesty and parliament to understand that, by fire and sword, to constrain princes and peoples to receive that one true religion of the gospel, is wholly against the mind and merciful law of Christ, dangerous both to king and state, a means to decrease the kingdom of Christ, and a means to increase the kingdom of antichrist. . . .

Even where physical coercion is not exerted upon dissenters to force their acceptance of the established religion, we fear that establishment is but the first step toward coercion of one kind or another, and to this we offer our unchanging objection. Robert Robinson saw the matter thus:

> No religion can be established without penal sanctions, and all penal sanctions in cases of religion are persecutions.

Before a man can persecute, he must renounce the generous tolerant dispositions of a Christian. No religion can be established without human creeds; and subscription to all human creeds implies two dispositions contrary to true religion, and both are expressly forbidden by the author of it. These two dispositions are, love of dominion over conscience, in the imposer, and an abject preference of slavery in the subscriber. The first usurps the rights of Christ; the last swears allegiance to a pretender. The first domineers, and gives laws like a tyrant; the last truckles like a vassal. The first assumes a dominion incompatible with his frailty, impossible even to his dignity, yet, denied to the dignity of angels; the last yields a low submission, inconsistent with his own dignity, and ruinous to that very religion, which he pretends by this mean to support.

The same anxiety which our British Baptist forefathers expressed in these and other pamphlets was felt by Baptists on this side of the Atlantic as well. Some of the settlers in the colonies had fled from England because of persecution, but these did not necessarily give up the idea of persecution in matters of religion, or of the establishment of religion under the power and sponsorship of government. It was only that in England they had seen the wrong religion established, and the wrong one persecuted. At this point their Baptist neighbors differed radically from them. Not only in colonial days, but in the days of the young American republic, Baptists were in the forefront of the company pleading for genuine religious liberty, to be guaranteed by the elimination of any religious establishment, whether that of the Church of England, or Congregationalism, or any other church. John Leland fought for this assurance both in Massachusetts and in Virginia. He announced his candidacy for membership in the Virginia convention to consider the proposed federal constitution, when it seemed possible that the new government would not sufficiently guarantee religious liberty, but withdrew in favor of

James Madison after Madison gave strong assurance of his own similar convictions in the matter.

For Leland this was no matter for merely academic discussion. His mother and brother had been imprisoned for refusing to pay a religious tax, and he wanted protections in the basic law of the land against any such compulsion in any case.

> Let every man speak freely without fear, maintain the principles that he believes, worship according to his own faith, either one God, three Gods, no God, or twenty Gods; and let government protect him in so doing, *i.e.*, see that he meets with no personal abuse, or loss of property, for his religious opinions.

These guarantees were written into the Bill of Rights, and Baptists may claim a share of the credit for having them there. We take these assurances to mean that none of the tax money collected from people of every religion and from those of no religion is to be used on behalf of any religious enterprise. Those who see no harm or danger in the use of public funds for worthy church activities may argue that this is a long way from religious persecution. Even this, however, compels the taxpayer to support a religious institution and to pay for religious instruction to which he does not give assent. To this extent it is a form of coercion in the realm of religion. Isaac Backus, pastor for half a century of the Baptist church at Middleborough, Massachusetts, argued the case in a resolution presented to the state assembly:

> Yet, as we are persuaded that an entire freedom from being taxed by civil rulers to religious worship, is not a mere favor, from any man or men in the world, but a right and property granted us by God, who commands us to stand fast in it, we have not only the same reason to refuse an acknowledgment of such a taxing power here, as America has the above-said power, but also, according to our present light, we

should wrong our consciences in allowing that power to men, which we believe belongs only to God.

Another corollary to our Baptist conviction about religious liberty is that no religious test should be applied for the purpose of admitting a person to public office, or of barring him from it. This kind of test is, in itself, a kind of establishment of religion. Discrimination on the basis of religious affiliation or nonaffiliation is a kind of persecution, even if it is not coupled with an attempt to apply physical coercion. The assessment of penalties of any kind by the state for religious opinions, or for the lack of them, is incompatible with the Christian gospel and, we believe, is equally incompatible with the noblest political ideals as well.

The "bloody tenet of persecution for conscience sake" is not yet a thing of the past. There are many countries in which religious liberty is still only a hope, and there are others where it is proclaimed, but its promises are not fulfilled. Baptists maintain an active interest in the effort to secure the rights of all men everywhere to practice their religion without persecution or interference. In those countries where there is a long-standing tradition of an established religion, of course, this will be achieved only through a gradual process. Yet, we are confident that this kind of liberty must accompany all others, lest all others be made a mockery. There is a spirit of freedom moving in the world today. It is expressed in the birth of new nations and in the death of colonialism. It is voiced in protests against totalitarianism. Demands for full rights of citizenship on the part of minority groups will not be silenced, and wherever these demands are heeded, the cause of religious freedom is advanced another step toward realization.

While we note with approval these signs of hope, we must remember that vexatious problems of church-state relationships remain even in our own American context. The constitutional guarantees of religious liberty do not solve these problems; indeed, they sometimes appear to make them more complex. Religious bodies are active in some of the realms in which various governmental agencies have a direct responsibility. The tasks of education of the young, care of the sick and aged, ministry to the needs of military personnel, medical research, and provision for welfare of the needy are matters of common concern to church and state. May the two cooperate in meeting these needs? Steps have been taken in recent years to give federal aid for the construction and maintenance of hospitals, and the funds provided are available to religious organizations as well as to state and local governments. As these words are being written our legislative leaders are struggling with problems connected with the grants of federal aid to education, both at the public school level and in higher education. Hardly a session of the United States Supreme Court passes without a request that the court pass on the constitutionality of some legislation relating to the use of tax moneys for institutions which belong to a church body. The courts are being faced with additional tests in an increasingly wide range of issues, requiring the most careful attention to minute details of methods of appropriation, use of funds, and precedents that have been established. The end is not in sight.

It should be confessed that, in some places, Baptist groups have themselves received some of these funds in ways that are, in the light of our historic principles, at least questionable. Some of our state conventions have leased, and are operating, hospitals built with funds from the Hill-Burton Act. Others, however, have sharply criticized this action, and have steadfastly refused to share in the provisions available through this legislation. It appears that some who have participated are recognizing a violation of principle in their action and are withdrawing as soon as their contractual arrangements can be terminated.

We have yet to work out the implications of our principles in these matters. There are areas in which church-related institutions are now eligible for assistance from public funds which were not dreamed of by our fathers. Low cost loans for dormitories, research grants, contracts for services rendered to the state or the federal government, grants of equipment, and "sale" of land and buildings at nominal cost —all these present to Baptists questions of policy which are of lasting importance. We cannot afford to answer them in terms of expediency or short-term gain, for they touch upon convictions that are basic to our way of life. It may be that the acceptance of some of these opportunities will not compromise the principles of religious liberty or endanger the separation of church and state. We cannot, however, solve the problem for ourselves on the ground that "everybody else is doing it." We first came out for religious liberty and the abolition of an established religion when "everybody else" was quite willing for the state to pay the church's way. We did not arrive at our convictions simply in order to be different, any more than we agreed to the common practice in order to be keeping up with everyone else. If we decide our position on these questions today in terms of any such superficial intention, we shall betray our ancestors and throw away their hard won gains. A considerable part of the world has learned to look to the Baptists for an unwavering stand for freedom and for the separation of the church and the state. It would be a tragedy of the gravest kind if we proved, in this generation, to be unable to give a clear and consistent witness to this fundamental conviction.

Some fear that a too-rigid policy in these matters will create a state which is the opposite of all for which Christians strive. They foresee, as the logical consequence of church-state separation, a thoroughly secularized society and the establishment of irreligion or anti-religion as the state's official policy. It was to avert this kind of conclusion that the Board of Regents in New York State composed a prayer which was prescribed for the public schools in that state. When, in 1962, the Supreme Court decided that this was unconstitutional, a great cry went up over the supposed endorsement of irreligion. Some Baptist voices joined in that cry. When, however, the ruling was more carefully read and more fully understood, it was seen that the Court had not "ruled God out of the public schools," as some had feared. Responsible Baptist leaders, among others, then began to acknowledge that the decision was in keeping with our tradition as a nation, as well as with our Baptist tradition. The government, and agencies of the government, of whatever kind, are simply warned that they are not to prescribe religious activities and impose them upon the citizens. In making this restriction upon governmental powers quite clear, the Court has underscored the affirmation of Baptists throughout the past three and one-half centuries.

We have been helped in the clarification of this and similar issues by the Baptist Joint Committee on Public Affairs, an agency with offices in Washington, supported by gifts from several general Baptist organizations. This committee gives invaluable assistance to the Baptist people by interpreting to them the issues which are before the Congress and in the courts, where church-state relations are involved. Another part of its work is the continuing discussion of the principles of religious liberty through various media, to encourage Baptists and others to give sustained attention to its preservation. Through conferences on religious liberty, federal aid to education, and similar topics, the committee draws together the wisdom and experience of people from all over the nation and provides a means of sharing insights and problems. Not least important is the committee's function in representing and interpreting the Baptist position on matters of public policy where church-state relations enter the picture. When congressional committees conduct hearings on proposed legislation involving these relations, the committee's staff members are available for presenting the hopes and concerns of the Baptist people. Through conferences and consultations we have been able to make our convictions known in an atmosphere of free discussion, and have been permitted to join forces with people of other denominations who share our insistence upon liberty of conscience.

We shall not be content with the securing of liberty for ourselves alone. It is a part of the conviction of Baptists concerning this precious possession that "so long as there is a man anywhere who hath not perfect liberty of conscience, I myself am part slave." Even at the risk of appearing to meddle in the affairs of other nations, we will continue to express our opposition to every restriction upon religious liberty in any country, whether applied in the name of religion, anti-religion, political stability, or social order. We will protest, too, against the limiting of this liberty to private worship or personal opinion. The Southern Baptist Convention in 1945 gave expression to the larger dimensions of liberty in the following statement:

> By this [i.e., religious liberty] we mean, and must mean, not only freedom of individual worship and fellowship without interference by the state; but we mean also specifically and insistently the right of propaganda through evangelism, education, and the development of Christian institutions. This we claim not as for ourselves, but for all men of all religious beliefs and of all theories of social order which are not obviously immoral or detrimental to the common welfare of men; and we demand this not as a concession or toleration, but as a basic right under God.

We rejoice in the gains for freedom in every place, not only in the realm of religious opinions and practices but in other realms as well. We receive strength, too, from those of other denominations who join with us in the struggle for freedom. The demand for religious liberty is not a Baptist monopoly. Our description of the contribution made by Baptists in this struggle is not an attempt to minimize the important contributions made by others. Indeed, we know that the safeguards which we seek will be achieved only if it is recognized that we are not advancing our own sectarian advantage, but the cause of the Christian community everywhere, and of all mankind.

Where liberty of conscience is allowed, then other freedoms will surely follow in time. Where it is denied, no other freedom can be assured. So long as Baptists have something significant to say to the world on behalf of this freedom in the realm of religion, we shall not need to be ashamed of the Baptist understanding of the Christian way.

INDEX